Marc GAILLARD

D1536564

The
"Arc de Triomphe"

English version by Nicola Randall

MARTELLE
É.D.I.T.I.O.N.S

Contents

PREFACE

Built between 1805 and 1835, with a ten-year break, the Arc de Triomphe, the Mecca of Paris, faces the Louvre but does not turn its back on La Défense. It stands on two avenues, which owe their elegance to their sweeping slopes. Its success is due, no doubt, to the life-size wooden and canvas framed model, paid for by the Town of Paris, made at the time when only four supports were sticking out of the ground, in order to nobly welcome the cortège of Napoleon and Marie-Louise, in 1810.

Which other architect in history ever had such opportunity at the very start of his work to modify, simplify, accentuate, reduce the high and low reliefs and thus improve the proportions ? I certainly know of none....

When one considers that each support bears a bulk equivalent in weight to around twice that of the Eiffel Tower, one can appreciate just how far architecture and engineering came during the 19th century, between the conception of the Arc de Triomphe in 1805 and that of the Eiffel Tower in 1889.

As the architect responsible for the conservation of the Arc de Triomphe over the past thirty years, and contrary to all expectations, I have had to undertake two pieces of restoration work, one in 1965 and the other in 1989. In 1965, as the monument had become as black as coal, we began with a general cleaning session and also replaced many large stones, sculpted or otherwise. In 1989 a few cracks began to appear which became particularly evident when a very small stone fell. Michel Bancon, a specialist in masonry analysis, was asked to carry out a very detailed technical study. He detected very slight subsidence on the Avenue Carnot side.

It was decided to reinforce the monument by incorporating a tie-rod superstructure and injecting into the foundations. This work took sixteen months. The erection of scaffolding meant that further cleaning work could also be carried out on the Arch.

The size, mass, weight, symmetry, simplicity, and cohesion of the monument together with all the details given by J.D. Thierry in his book of 1845, taught us a sound lesson in architecture and, to be more precise, in stability for both the work projects. As a result it was possible to test out new control, maintenance and reinforcement techniques more easily than would have been possible elsewhere ; this experience came in useful for other buildings.

The two projects lead us to consult the Archives Nationales et Parisiennes.

At the Archives Nationales, a graphic representation of the work, layer by layer, stone by stone, for the ten years that it took to complete the Arch, shows just how seriously the architects and members of the building trade took their work during this period. At the Bibliothèque Historique de la Ville de Paris, the one hundred watercolours painted on a scale of 1 : 200 by J.D. Thierry, Inspector of the Arc de Triomphe, prior to his engravings for a book, so impressed me that in 1990 I began to dream of using them to put together a book about the Arch. I did not have the time. I am glad that Marc Gaillard was able to take on this task.

Michel MAROT
Chief Architect of Civil Buildings and National Palaces

CLASSIC AND MODERN ROMAN TRIUMPHAL ARCHES

In Ancient Times triumphal arches were only found in the Roman world, but the Roman Empire aspired to universal influence ; for several centuries it succeeded in imposing Latin civilisation on many parts of the world, in the belief that this was superior because it had descended from the Greeks and was based on all forms of culture and art. Latin civilisation spread to Europe, a part of Asia Minor and areas of Africa around the Mediterranean, before meeting with the barbaric ways of nomadic and primitive people.

Certain forms of tribute were deemed indispensable to the glorification of the Republic, notably the construction of triumphal arches in honour of conquering warriors. The first arches were made of wood, later ones of stone, possibly of brick like the arch built in honour of Romulus. In time arches were to become genuine, important monuments constructed in freestone, decorated with pillars, raised up on sculpted horses or other allegories, and fully or partially covered by high or low relief sculptures with inscriptions telling of the warriors' glorious battles.

In the Roman Empire arches were found not only in the forum but also at the entrance to a town and on main communication routes. Rome constructed many triumphal arches and most of these still exist today, although some are in a state of near ruin.

Arch of Constantine, built in 312. Painting, Romantic era.

Prior to this, the Estruscans had built "Fornix" or "Fornice", arch-shaped constructions, into the walls of their city entrances.

Some three hundred and sixty triumphal entrances were constructed in Rome, temporary arches through which the armies passed.

The very first monumental arch was that of Augustus in the Forum, the foundations of which still exist today, near to

*Triumphal Arch
of Septimius Severus
in a Roman forum
in Leptis Magna, Libya.*

*Triumphal Arch
in Timgad dedicated
to Trajan.*

Caesar's Temple. It was erected in 39 BC to celebrate the victory of Actium in Greece in the year 31, a naval defeat by Octavius and Agrippa over Anthony and Cleopatra's army, which guaranteed Octavian domination of the ancient world.

Two gates dating back to the 3rd and 2nd centuries BC still exist at Perouse, one of which is the Gate of Mars. In the centuries to follow, a number of "Gates of Mars" were erected, the most famous of which in France is that of Rheims. Others could be found at Autun, Saintes, Nîmes, Saint-Rémy de Provence, Saint-Chamas, Cavaillon, Langres, Trier and Alcantara in Spain.

Arches dedicated to Augustus (emperor from 27 BC to 14 AD) can still be found today in Rome, Aosta, Fano, Rimini and Susa. Arches dedicated to Trajan (emperor from 98 to 117) can be seen in Ancona, Bari, Benevento, Maktar, Merida and Timgad. Others to Septimius Severus (emperor from 193 to 211) still stand in Dougga, Haidra, Lambese, Leptis-Magna and Rome while ones built in tribute to Caracalla, (emperor from 211 to 217) are to be found in Djemilla, Thassos, Tebessa and Volubilis.

The arch of Titus in the forum of Rome is an arch with a single opening. The high reliefs represent Titus on his chariot pulled by a team of four horses and tell the story of how Judaea was defeated.

The arch of Septimius Severus, also in Rome, recalls this emperor's victory over the Parthians. The triumphal arch of Timgad in Algeria is a solemn reminder of the founding of a colony, just like the one at Orange which is one of the largest Roman arches : 20 metres wide, 8 metres deep and 19 metres high. Its high reliefs, now badly eroded, portray the legions' battles against the Gauls.

The arch of Germanicus in Saintes commemorates the completion of the Roman road from Lyon to Saintes (Julius Caesar Germanicus was a Roman general, grand-

Triumphal Arch in Benevent, built in 114, dedicated to Trajan. The high reliefs depict the story of Augustus.

Arch of Titus in Rome

nephew of Augustus, adopted by Tiberius ; he conquered Arminius in Germania in the year 16).

The arch of Janus in Rome was a tetrapyle arch, in other words it had four openings, one in each side, a principle which was used by Chalgrin for the triumphal arch of the Great Army in Paris, but which could also be found in ancient times in Tripoli and Leptis Magna in Libya, at Tebassa in Algeria, and at Apamie, Basra, Damascus, Palmyra, Shabba and Latakia in Syria.

The Arch of Trajan in Benevento was erected in 114 by the architect Apollodore of Damascus at the time when this emperor was at war with the Parthians, a people allied with the Scythe people settled in northern Iran and in Mesopotamia. The marble high reliefs extol the story of Augustus, who was considered to be one of the greatest emperors of all time.

Augustus (63 BC to 14 AD), grandnephew and also heir of Julius Caesar, won fame at the naval battle of Astium in Greece. He created organs of government, civil service bodies, rebuilt Rome and its provinces and reinforced its system of centralized government. A smart and masterful man, he was looked upon as a god after his death. His rule is seen as one of the major eras in the history of Rome. In this respect one talks about the "Century of Augustus".

The Arch of Glanum, near Saint-Rémy de Provence, is a triumphal arch with only one archway and, although this is now badly damaged, its decorative high reliefs and rounded forms can still be recognised. It was to inspire differing projects for the Arc de Triomphe in Paris. It was dedicated to Marcus Aurelius (emperor from 121 to 180) who also fought against the Parthians. This philosophical prince gave a share of his power to his son Commodus. He tolerated all religions — except Christianity. An arch dedicated to

Marcus Aurelius can also be found in Djemilla (or Djemilah).

The Arch of Septimius Severus at Leptis-Magna, birthplace of this emperor who ruled from 193 to 211, is now badly deteriorated. It too was an arch with three openings. Another arch was dedicated to him in Rome, to celebrate his victory over the Parthians, and this also had three openings with projecting columns. It was to inspire the Arch of Constantine in the following century.

At the very top was a chariot pulled by six horses. Septimius Severus was accompanied by his sons Caracalla and Gea. This arch was also elaborately sculpted on all four sides.

The Arch of Constantine in Rome is both the last and the largest of the Empire's arches. It is 25 metres wide, 6.5 metres deep and 20 metres high, 12 metres in the centre and 6 metres at the sides. It was built in the 4th century. It is an arch with three openings.

The story of Constantine's victories is told on the frieze. The arch also portrays Marcus Aurelius, Hadrian and Trajan. It is the best know of all Rome's triumphal arches because of the drawings and copies made of it and the Empire by the Renaissance architects Serlio and Palladio. Léonard Fontaine, together with his fellow-architect Percier, was inspired by it for his Carrousel Arch, with its projecting columns and warriors on the cornices. Marble Arch in England, near to Buckingham Palace, built by John Nash in 1828, was also inspired by this arch.

Constantine 1st, known as Constantine The Great, (emperor from 280 to 337) was the son of Constantius Chlorus whom he succeeded. He permitted freedom of worship and allowed Christianity to triumph in the West. In 325 he convened the first Synod at Nicea. In 324-330 he founded the new Rome of the East : Constantinople.

Adrian's Arch in Athens is a fairly mo-

*Arch of Septimius Severus
in Rome*

*Arch of Constantine in Rome,
main façade*

dest construction not far from the ancient port of Piraeus. Adrian, or Hadrian (76 - 138) was Trajan's successor. He reformed the administrative system and was responsible for the building of a fortification against barbaric invasions : Hadrian's Wall in Germania.

The Romans used many differing geometrical designs on their numerous triumphal arches, having experimented with a whole range of architectural possibilities. Roman engineers and architects had already worked out the principle of an arch or an arcade in the 2nd century BC. There were no arches in either Egypt or Greece before this period. All sorts of design can be incorporated into an arch, it can be accompanied, or not, by secondary arcades, columns, pilasters, sculpted piedroits or simply drafted.

The simplest type of triumphal arch has only one archway. If a triumphal arch is also to serve as an entranceway to the town, as in Autun, Reims, Trier, etc, side archways are also added. That of Trier, 30 metres tall, was erected at the time of Septimius Severus. Triumphal arches with a triple opening are less common but more monumental in style. That in Orange is the oldest of this kind in France.

An arch with four bays - also known as "quadriphone" or "tetrapyle" or "Janus" because the arch dedicated to Janus, the God of Gates, was the first to be built in this way in Rome — is the least common and the most monumental ; the result is four different perspectives, such as exists at the Arc de l'Etoile.

It can be noted that the Carrousel Arch is a triple bay arch, coupled with a tetrapyle arch. It has, therefore, five openings, three on the main axis and two on the perpendicular axis.

From the time of the Renaissance period, following studies and copied drawings of Roman arches — notably the Constantine Arch — published by the famous architects Serlio and Palladio, temporary triumphal arches started to appear in Europe. These consisted generally of a large wooden portico with stucco, sometimes covered with painted canvas to simulate architecture, through which dazzling processions of kings, emperors or lesser monarchs passed.

So it was that in 1574, King Henry the 3rd, short lived monarch of Poland, passed through an arch which had been built by Palladio, during a brief visit to Venice. It was a framework arch, an imitation of the Constantine Arch, but some of the painted canvas was done by the hand of Tintoret or Veronese.

Thirty years prior to this, in 1540, Catherine of Medicis and King Henry 2nd were greeted in Lyon. Four triumphal arches were erected for the occasion. In 1600, Marie of Medicis journeyed through this same town and the royal procession passed under four arches, which had been built for the event. Evidently Lyon had no intention of skimping on such matters.

When she was exiled in 1638, Marie of Medicis was received in Amsterdam under an arch commissioned by the Prince of Orange.

In 1635 Antwerp was to welcome Archduke Ferdinand of Austria. The aldermen of the town called upon Rubens and Jordaens to paint the canvas for the triumphal arch.

In the middle of the previous century the town of Brussels had commissioned a wonderfully decorated arch to be erected to receive Philip 2nd of Spain. Antwerp, Gent, Bruges and Leuven copied Brussels for this same princely visit and the town corporations constructed buildings of a similar style.

In London in 1533, Hans Holbein was responsible for decorating the arch that had been erected for Anne Boleyn's coronation. At Messina, in 1535 the Caravage decorated an arch.

Sangallo in Rome and Peruzzi in Siena

Arch of Orange

Arch of Glanum (St Rémy-de-Provence)

carried out decorative work on the occasion of Charles Quint's visit. In England, in 1602, the painter Inigo Jones reconstituted the Constantine Arch in wood and painted canvas for the coronation of James the 1st.

In Spain, still in honour of Charles Quint, further temporary arches were erected.

In France, on 26th August, 1660, for the arrival in Paris of Louis 14th and Maria Theresa of Austria, the Spanish Infanta, a superb, three-arched triumphal arch, magnificently decorated with statues and high reliefs, based on Le Brun's drawings, was erected in the Place du Trône. Poussin and van Ostade assisted with the painted decorative work.

A second arch was put up in Rue Saint-Antoine, a third in Rue de la Truanderie, yet another on the Notre-Dame bridge, whilst a fifth closed off Place Dauphine opposite the terreplein of Pont Neuf.

The reign of Louis 14th was to leave Paris with the two triumphal arches that we now know as Porte Saint-Martin and Porte Saint-Denis. The architect Nicolas François Blondel built the latter in 1672, at the town's expense, to celebrate the king's victories in the Rhine area of Germany and in Flanders.

In 1674, the arch known as the Porte Saint-Martin was erected from drawings by Blondel and Pierre Bullet to commemorate the capture of Besançon and victory over the German, Spanish and Dutch armies.

Porte Saint-Denis in Paris.
Painting by Kojiro Akagi.

The old Saint-Antoine gates at the north side of the Bastille, and Saint Bernard on the Quai de la Tournelle, which were also true triumphal arches, disappeared shortly before the Revolution. They too were the work of Nicolas François Blondel.

In 1667, Colbert had asked the architect Claude Perrault to design a triumphal arch for the Place du Trône.

The plans envisaged a monument of considerable size — 50 metres high and

Temporary Triumphal Arch, Place du Trône. Arrival of Louis 14th and Queen Marie-Thérèse.

Triumphal Arch of Porte Saint-Denis in 1683. Drawing by Perelle.
Blondel's Arch is seen here from the suburb of Saint-Denis.

56 metres wide with three arches and a statue of Louis 14th mounted on horseback. A framework model with painted canvas was made but that was as far as the project went.

Between 1686 and 1695 the architect Simon Volland built another arch in Lille to the glory of Louis 14th. This is today called the "Paris" Gate.

In Montpellier, François d'Orbey and Auguste Daviler built the Peyrou Arch, once again to the glory of Louis 14th.

In Bordeaux, in 1748, the architect Nicolas Poitier built the Dijeaux Gate. The Aquitaine and Salinière Gates in this same town are both monumental entrances in the form of a triumphal arch.

At Chalons-sur-Marne the arch of the Sainte-Croix Gate was built to welcome the Archduchess of Austria, Marie-Antoinette, the new Queen of France, on her arrival.

In 1783 work started on the "Porte Guillaume" arch in Dijon in honour of the Prince de Condé, Governor of Burgundy.

In Nancy, Emmanuel Héré, responsible for Place Stanislas and the Place de la Carrière, erected between 1754 and 1756 the triumphal arch which separated these two beautiful squares. Other monumental gates had been built in this town : the Gate of Saint Nicolas, 1603 - 1608, with two arches ; the Gate of Sainte-Catherine with three arches, in 1752 ; and the Gate of Stanislas, also in 1752, the work of the architect Richard Mique, a pupil of Héré. The Gate of Desilles, Cours Leopold, was built in 1785.

In Italy the most important «modern» triumphal arch is that in Florence, built in 1739 in honour of the Great Duke François 3rd of Lorraine.

In Madrid, the Puerta de Alcada, with five arches, was built in 1778 by Francisco Sabatini.

In Berlin, the architect Friedrich Gilly contemplated building a huge tetrapyle

Porte Saint-Martin Triumphal Arch. Painting by Hubert Robert. 1770.

Transformation of the Porte Saint-Martin by the architect François Blondel. Return of Louis 15th after the Battle of Fontenoy.

*Plan of a triumphal arch
in Toulon harbour (1793).*

*Plan of the Sans-culottes Arch
by Boullée.*

arch to the glory of Frederick 2nd, but this was never built.

In France, the visionary architects Etienne Louis Boullée and Antoine Voinier designed, from 1780, huge triumphal arches so ornately decorated with forests of pillars and quadriges that they had little hope of ever actually being built.

The revolutionaries who regarded the triumphal arches of Louis 14th as symbols of "absolutism" suggested that the Portes Saint-Denis and Saint Martin be had in fact initially intended to build two porticos in the form of a triumphal arch surrounded by colonnades, placed on Rue Vivienne.

In 1794 Antoine Voinier put forward ideas for a colossal building dedicated to the armies of the Republic, to be built on Chaillot Hill, in other words on the site of the present day Arc de Triomphe.

For Chaillot Hill, Philibert Moitte envisaged an arch with pillars supported by

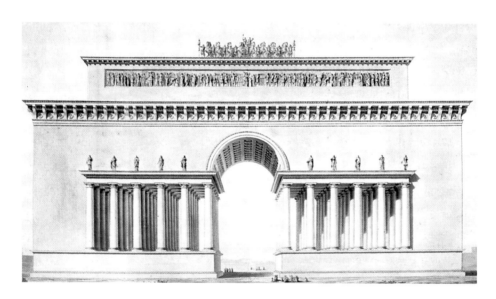

Lequeu and Boulée : plan of a colossal triumphal arch in Paris.

transformed. In 1790, a large 25-metre framework arch, with three archways of the same height, was built at the Champ de Mars for the Fête de la Fédération, on the site later to be occupied by the Eiffel Tower.

Alexandre Brongniart, who was to construct the Bourse, designed an "Arc des Sans Culottes", dedicated to the "martyrs for freedom", followed by an "Arc des Quatre Saisons".

In his plans for the Bourse, Brogniart eighteen elephants and a victory symbol accompanied by eight lions.

Triumphal arches were becoming the height of fashion. Jean Nicolas Sobre imagined one for the Pont de la Concorde. Yet another was erected in 1792 at the start of the Champs Elysées with a semicircle of colonnades around the Marly horses.

Jean-Jacques Lequeu, another architect of great vision, envisaged a triumphal

Portico entrance in the shape of a triumphal arch. Hotel Théluson, 1780 (Rue de Provence, former Rue d'Artois).

Plan of a colossal arch for Chaillot Hill facing the Champs Elysées, by Voinier. Glorification of the Armies of the 1st Republic, 1794.

arch to be named the "People's Arch" or the "Gate of Paris".

In 1805 Napoleon finally decreed that a triumphal arch should be built at the top of the Champs Elysées Avenue.

Other triumphal arches were built in Europe and around the world in the 19th century. We must mention the one built in the main square of Milan in 1803, the Gate of Moscow built in Leningrad in 1814, the War Memorial Arch built in New Delhi in 1833 and the Memorial Arch in New York in 1899.

The Brandenburg Gate of Berlin is older since it was built in 1789 by the architect Carl Laughaus. It is crowned by a copper quadrige.

In Madrid the Gate of Toledo dates back to 1813, the triumphal arch of the Etad Major to 1819. The Neva Gate in Leningrad is from 1829.

In London, Wellington Arch and Marble Arch date from 1828. In Moscow the arch known as the Arch of Tserskevtov was built in 1834.

In Lisbon the "Commerce Square Gate" is also a three-passage arch, built between 1843 and 1873. The Arch of Victor Pradera in Barcelona was constructed in 1888 ; the "Monument to the Revolution" in Mexico in 1902. In Bombay the Gate of India with its three arcades dates from 1911.

In Berlin Hitler commissioned the architect Speer to build a gigantic arch but this work was never carried out.

In Italy Mussolini commissioned two arches to be built, one in Genes in 1931 to honour those who had died in the First World War and the other in Bolzano in Upper Adige, the "Arco della Vittoria".

In 1936 in Madrid, General Franco had an arch built with a single opening.

In Teheran, Iran, Shah Mohammed Reza Palawi had a superb, 45-metre high tetrapyle arch built in reinforced, but nonetheless very elegant, concrete. This was the monument of Schahyad. At Saint-

Temporary Triumphal Arch constructed at the Barrière de Pantin in 1807. Return of Napoleon after the Prussian Campaign.

Carrousel Triumphal Arch celebrating
victory at Austerlitz.
Above : Peace riding on its Triumphal
Chariot, by François Joseph Bosio.
Below : Watercolour by Galien Laloue
in 1910.

Louis in Missouri, the architect Eero Saarinen completed a huge elliptical arch of exceptional elegance in front of the Jefferson National Expansion Memorial. We must not forget either the Monument aux Morts d'Orient built in Marseilles in 1927 at one end of the Avenue de Prado, looking out to sea. The architect Castel built this triumphal arch.

In this same town, the architect Penchaud, with the help of the sculptor David d'Angers had built the Gate of Aix at the time of Louis Philippe. It is one of the most beautiful 19th century monuments of its kind.

Designed by the Danish architect Otto von Sprekelson, the great Arche de la Défense, is the third triumphal arch in Paris to make a mark in history as seen by Le Nostre in the 17th century, beginning in the court of Napoleon 3rd in the Louvre and of which the first monumental part is the Carrousel triumphal arch.

Right-hand page : Triumphal Arch of the Palais Longchamp in Marseille celebrating the arrival of the Eaux de la Durance.

At the beginning of this century and during the Thirties, several other forms of archway and monumental arch were envisaged which would mark the historical axis between Porte Maillot and La Défense, including that of architect Robert Mallet-Stevens at Porte Maillot in 1929, those of the architects Lesage and Miltgen at La Défense in 1931 and that of Yeo Ming Peï at the same place in 1971.

Triumphal Arch known as "La Porte d'Aix" in Marseilles, inspired by the Arch of Titus, built between 1834 and 1839.

THE "ARC DE TRIOMPHE DE L'ÉTOILE"

UTOPIAN IDEAS AND PLANS

The idea of erecting a grand monument on Chaillot Hill, which could be seen from the Champs Elysées, had already been considered well before the Arc de Triomphe.

In 1723 Evrard Tillon du Tillet, author of a study on the great French poets and musicians, suggested building a monument dedicated to the "Parnasse Français" on Chaillot Hill, a grandiose sculpture of which the original drawings by Audran can be seen in the Bibliothèque Nationale. The monument, 160 feet (50 metres) wide and 60 feet (20 metres) tall, was built in the shape of a pyramid, a composition dominated by a spirit on horseback at the top of it.

The Marquis of Marigny, under Louis 15th, had plans for marking the centre of the Chaillot circus with an obelisk in white marble but this was never built.

In 1758 Jean-Etienne Ribart, an engineer and member of the Béziers Académie des Sciences et Lettres presented King Louis 15th with plans which were particularly ambitious : a colossal elephant containing various concert and dance rooms and even suites for visiting foreign officials. A grand stairway was to occupy the centre of the building. On its back the elephant was to carry a huge palanquin in which would be enthroned an equally monumental royal allegorical effigy, surrounded by flags and lions lying down. Powerful jets of water would spray from the elephant's trunk directed into basins and lakes placed around the elephant, with another lake and a canal on the Champs Elysées side.

Louis 15th did not take the project up, considering that his victories bore no relation to those of Hannibal... Nevertheless Jean-Etienne Ribart's elephant was to serve as an inspiration for later projects... that of Philibert Moitte, for instance, with its pedestal of elephants and its crown of lions.

In 1789, the Minister of the Interior, François de Neuchâteau, responsible for setting up international exhibitions of industrial products, ran a competition. Thirteen projects were looked into the following year, but in fact none ever went any further.

In 1802 the architect Balzac (no relation to the great novelist) designed an arch shaped like a huge semicircular curve, showing at its colossal keystone a man holding a Victory and above it the words "Paix Générale An X".

Other projects began to appear such as, in 1809, that of Avrilliet and Grange, with a large arch and two passages, and projecting Corinthian columns showing figures of people and a crown of canons and flags.

In 1819, Dubois designed a sort of temple dedicated to the glory of Napoleon. In 1812, it was the turn of Baltard (father of the architect des Halles) to put forward different projects, all elaborately decorated with sculptures. Let us not forget either, and they were certainly not to be the last, the work of the architects Médous and Chauvin...

When work halted during the Restoration period, another project began, in addition to that of Louis Bruyère already mentioned, that of a huge columned building in honour of the country's great men and distinguished kings. In 1823, Edme Gaulle presented two sets of plans, which included quadrigas and horsemen. Marie-Antoine Carême, the famous chef of Talleyrand, presented one way in which the arch could be completed in his book : Projets pour les Embellissements de Paris et de Saint-Pétersbourg.

In 1824 the architect Huyot, together with Goust, took the work up again ; he drew up two sets of plans for the façades, one without columns, and the other with. Goust was also to present a new design with projecting Corinthian columns. Huyot's plans, with their statues placed in

Plan of a triumphal arch with pedestal consisting of elephants and a crown made up of lions. Philibert Moitte, 1795.

Below right : Plan of a triumphal arch for the Paix Générale, by Balzac in the year X (1802).

Plan of a monumental elephant bearing a statue of Louis XV for Etoile Hill on Champs Elysées side. Jean Etienne Ribart de Chamoust, 1758.

recesses or on the upper balustrade, were not accepted, neither were those of Goust.

By now Napoleon had now decided that a triumphal arch should be built in Paris to honour the Great Army and the question of the best position for this great building in the capital began to be hotly debated. Each architect had his own ideas concerning the ideal site : les Gobelins, la Barrière d'Italie, le Pont d'Austerlitz, la Barrière d'Enfer, la Bastille, le Champ de Mars, la Colline or" l'Etoile de Chaillot...

As far as the new Minister of the Interior, Nompére de Champagny, was concerned, there could be only one place : Chaillot Hill. He skilfully explained to the Emperor all the reasons why this site was preferable tò the others.

"This place could be described as one of the most beautiful quarters of Paris since it joins the Champs Elysées by way of a walkway. A triumphal arch at the Etoile would finish off in a most majestic and picturesque way the superb view that one has of the imperial Château des Tuileries. In this position, the monument would be visible from very far away and would hinder no view. It could be seen from the heights of Neuilly and from the Place de la Concorde. It would attract the admiration of any traveller entering Paris, since monuments of this kind have most effect when seen from afar, leaving more to the imagination."

Your Majesty would pass by it on the way to La Malmaison, Saint-Germain or Versailles by whichever road he may care to take through the Bois.

The Barrière de l'Etoile is visited by all classes of citizens, who go there to breathe in the country air on bank holidays and to relax as they walk along the public pathway closest to Paris, the Bois de Boulogne."

On 14th May 1806 Napoleon sent a note to Champagny from Saint-Cloud saying :

"Triumphal arches would be pointless pieces of work, serving little purpose, if they were not a means of encouraging architecture." Napoleon therefore contemplated four arches in Paris. *"One has to be the Marengo Arch, another the Austerlitz Arch, a third the Arc de Triomphe de la Paix and a fourth the Arc de Triomphe de la Religion. By these four arches I mean to keep sculpture in France going for another twenty years..."*

In 1806 the Minister of the Interior organised a competition but without result. The Emperor therefore saw to the urgent start of work on the Arc de Triomphe de la Grande Armée. The work was entrusted to Chalgrin and Raymond, architect members of the Institute.

Work began immediately on digging the eight metre deep excavations needed for the foundation. The first two courses were set in place around the perimeter of the monument.

On 15th August 1806 the "first stone" was set in the centre, between two pillars, on the Passy side.

This hexagonal slab measuring 3.65 metres by 1.60 metres was of considerable size and is to be found deep below the monument. It bears an inscription covered with a strip of lead to protect it from the effects of the weather :

« L'AN 1806, LE QUINZIÈME D'AOÛT, JOUR ANNIVERSAIRE DE LA NAISSANCE DE SA MAJESTÉ NAPOLÉON LE GRAND, CETTE PIERRE EST LA PREMIÈRE QUI AIT ÉTÉ POSÉE DANS LA FONDATION DE CE MONUMENT ».

"This first stone", states François de Saint-Simon in his outstanding study on the Place de l'Etoile, "was set in place without official ceremony, on the initiative of the workers themselves."

At the same time as the foundations were being dug, architects were working on plans for the façades. Jean-François Chalgrin suggested grand projecting Corinthian columns, similar to those of the Constantine Arch in Rome ; Raymond

Pilot-studies for the Arc
de Triomphe de la Grande
Armée by J.-B. Chalgrin.
Nicolas Huyot ;
Raymond Blouet
and the "Commission"
of Governmental Architects.

opted for columns set into the stonework. Many varied ideas were put forward.

By the end of 1807, the foundations were nearly finished. All that was left to do was to place a course at ground level. The work had been carried out speedily. Exceptionally strong stone from the Château-Landon quarries of the Vallée du Loing had been used. To save money the Emperor decided against the columns which had been suggested by the architects and ordered the main arch to be made smaller. In the end, the arch was limited to the size originally suggested, 14.6 metres by 29.4 metres high, the side arches being 18 metres high by 8.5 metres wide.

In March 1808, Raymond presented a new project to the Minister of the Interior and this was accepted by Napoleon, although the Victory statues, which were to have decorated the projecting base, were abandoned, again because of financial misgivings.

On 31st October, Jean-François Chalgrin was appointed sole architect of the monument in an attempt to avoid time-wasting discussions with his fellow architects. So it was that at the end of 1808 he presented new plans, this time without columns, and it was more or less these that were followed once work began.

Contrary to the Emperor's expectations, the estimated cost for this work was finally put at 9,132,000 francs, as opposed to the 7,292,000 francs quoted for the first project with columns. This additional cost was the result of extending all the high reliefs and sculpted parts, originally planned to be in marble, and the choice of hard stone from Château-Landon, which Chalgrin wished to see used for the entire facing of the building. Indeed it was this stone from the Vallée de Loing, in the Nemours area, that was used for the pillars and openings right up to the keystone of the great arch.

1808 saw the opening of the new Château-Landon quarry, which held work up somewhat. Chalgrin's plans were conclusively approved on 27th March 1809, and work on the site was speeded up.

However, in 1810 an event took place which enabled Chalgrin (who was to die the following year), to see his triumphal arch "virtually" completed.

Indeed Napoleon had just married the daughter of the Germanic Emperor François 2nd of Austria and the Archduchess Marie-Louise of Habsbourg Lorraine. The marriage had been concluded in Vienna on 7th February 1810. The official ceremony was to take place on 1st April at Saint-Cloud, following which the sovereigns were to make a solemn entrance into Paris before the religious consecration planned to take place in the Palais de Tuileries.

Chalgrin had to act quickly to build a framework arch, covered in painted canvas to make it look like the finished arch, through which the procession could pass on their way from Saint Cloud.

Five hundred workers were employed by the architect and they made the most of the situation by going on strike and demanding two pay rises. These they received but not before being threatened with reprisals by the Minister of the Interior. The carpenters, who were paid 4 francs a day, demanded to be paid 9, and this was accepted, then 18, which they also received and finally 24. It was at this point that the Préfet de Police Dubois stepped in : six workers were arrested and the demands ceased.

Chalgrin called upon the painter Laffitte to do the trompe-l'œil decor work. In his workshop in Rue de Tournon, Laffitte managed to work miracles and in only twenty or so days, with many helpers, produced the whole set of painted canvases. The results were judged to be "superb".

The temporary triumphal arch cost 511,000 francs, including 21,500 for the

Fireworks celebrating the marriage of the Emperor to Marie-Louise of Austria in 1810.

Temporary Arc de Triomphe and tollgates in 1810. Lithograph by Garbizza.

painted canvas. At the same time Chalgrin was able to correct certain flaws in his plans. He decided to do away with the pedestals on the façade side and to place greater emphasis on the main façades by placing them exactly in line with the supports. Indeed this is what was later done.

On the four panels to either side of the main arch on the Paris and Neuilly sides, the themes developed by the painter Laffitte on his canvases were *"Les Embellissements de Paris présentés a l'Empereur"* ; *"La Clémence de l'Empereur couronné par la Victoire"* ; and *"Le Code Napoléon offert aux Législateurs"*.

At the top, four friezes showed, on the Ternes side : *"L'Arrivée de l'Archiduchesse à Paris"* ; on the Passy side : *"L'Alliance de leurs Majestés et leurs Majestés sur le Trône impérial"*; and on the attic of the Paris side, was written the inscription : *"A Napoléon et à Marie-Louise, la Ville de Paris"*.

On 1st April 1810 the imperial cortège was the first in a long line to pass through the Arc de Triomphe. The coach, drawn by eight horses, was proceeded by the Garde and followed by one hundred carriages carrying members of the imperial family, ministers, dignitaries of the Empire and ambassadors.

A large crowd had gathered in the square around the arch and on the surrounding hills (today Rue Lauriston) and, of course, along the Champs Elysées as far as the gates of the Tuileries where Fontaine had constructed a second triumphal arch with triple openings.

Jean-François Chalgrin died on 20th January 1811, having completed all his plans, drawings and cross-sections of the monument. Work continued under his pupil Goust, who had previously been an inspector of works.

He was appointed architect of the building on 1st May 1811 and was to stick ri-

Jean-François CHALGRIN (1739-1811) was a pupil of the famous Servandoni, designer of the Saint-Sulpice façade and plans for the square of the same name. Creator of numerous pieces of trompe-l'oeil decor for the theatre as well as for very many palaces and castles throughout Europe, Chalgrin was also taught by Etienne Boullée who, as a reaction against the Baroque style of the Louis 15th period, advocated a return to ancient simplicity, which resulted in fact in the style of Louis 16th. He was also a disciple of Claude Nicolas Ledoux.

Jean-François Chalgrin was the winner of the Grand Prix de Rome in 1758, a member of the Académie d'Architecture in 1770 and a member of L'Institut in 1799.

He built the sacristy of Besançon Cathedral in 1771 and, subsequently, the façade of the Château de Surville, near Montereau, the Collège de France, the Château de Brunoy, the Pavillon de Musique de Madame in Versailles (in 1784), the Hôtel du Compte de Saint-Florentin in Paris — today the United States Consulate — on the corner of Rues de Rivoli and Saint-Florentin, in 1767, the church of Saint-Philippe du Roule, between 1774 and 1784, the north tower of Saint-Sulpice, the Chapelle du Saint-Esprit — Rue Lhomond — the Escalier d'Honneur du Luxembourg and its vestibule. He was appointed sole architect of the Arc de Triomphe in 1808.

Chalgrin did not have time to take work on the Arc de Triomphe very far ; nonetheless paternity for the monument is attributed to him.

Jean-Arnaud RAYMOND (1742-1811) was born in Toulouse. In Paris he was a pupil of Jacques-François Blondel (1705-1774), responsible for famous architectural treaties, who practised his profession mostly in Metz and Strasbourg.

As he was only able to work on the Arc de Triomphe — in collaboration with Chalgrin — as far as the foundation level, Raymond worked mostly in the Languedoc, in Nîmes and Montpellier.

*Two other plans for
the Arc de Triomphe
by Chalgrin and Raymond.*

gidly to Calgrin's plans until the year 1813.

The four pillars now reached a height of 19.6 metres, in other words to the level of the course on which the vault of the great arch was to rest. The small arches were finished, including the decor sculpted with roses and caissons.

Work was interrupted in 1814. The architect Guillaume Poyet, incidentally a most talented man (he was responsible for constructing the façade of the Bourbon palace), suggested razing the pillars of the arch. Fortunately Louis 18th paid no heed to what he said.

For nearly ten years things remained as they were. In 1823 the engineer Bruyère, director of works in Paris, appointed at this time to finish the Ourcq canal, suggested transforming the unfinished arch into a water tower fed from the Bassin de la Villette, with a statue of Neptune at the top surrounded by tritons and, at its foot, fountains with nymphs and many jets of water.

Numerous and no less extravagant suggestions, which would have entailed substantial work, had already preceded this project, which itself was not to be the last...

Cross section of the large east-west axis.

Cross-section of the south-west pillars.

"He wandered on lost in thought, he walked on, looking at the monuments in Place Louis 15th. It was a fine day. A stream of beautiful carriages drove by him heading for the great Avenue des Champs Elysées. He followed the crowds and saw the three or four thousand coaches that could always be found driving around there on any beautiful Sunday, making a real Longchamp of it. Overcome by the sheer luxury of the horses, their grooming, their livery, he kept on going until he found himself in front of the Arc de Triomphe"

Honoré de Balzac. *Les Illusions perdues.*

Cross section of the north-south transverse axis with scaffolding.

Cross section of the north-south axis.

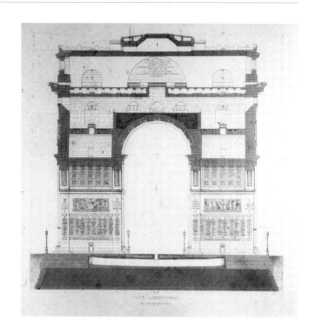

Cross section of the north-south axis showing rooms in the upper part

Cross-section of the east-west axis with scaffolding.

Jean-Nicolas Huyot. Born in Paris on 25th December 1780, this architect and archaeologist came from a building family, his father was an architect and contractor. At first he considered a career in engineering and began preparing for the entrance exam to the Ecole Polytechnique, but never took the exam, having suddenly decided that he wanted to become a painter and enrolled in the workshop of the famous Louis David. He remained there for several years before turning towards architecture and he became of pupil of Antoine François Peyre. In 1807 he won the first Grand Prix de Rome. He therefore left for Italy like all "Prix de Rome" winners, and stayed in Rome for five years at Villa Médicis where, in 1804, he set up the "Académie de France à Rome", which still occupies this magnificent palace today.

In Rome, Huyot made copies and drawings of ancient triumphal arches : Septimius Severus, Constantine, Titus, the Major Gate, the Temples of Janus and Drusus, the Temple of Fortune at Palestrina, etc.

On his return to France in 1813, he was appointed governmental inspector of works. The Earl of Forbin-Janson (1777-1841), painter, archaeologist, member of the Academy and Director of the Musées Royaux under Louis 13th and Charles 10th, invited Jean Nicolas Huyot to take part in major archaeological explorations of Greece, Constantinople, the Aegean Sea, Syria and Egypt. The journey began on 22nd August 1817. The first stop was the island of Milos where Huyot broke his leg. He had to spend some time in hospital and whilst there he did many drawings, notably of ancient ruins of which there were a considerable number at this time.

He visited Ephesus and then travelled on to Constantinople where he made further drawings before embarking for Alexandria and Egypt where he made studies of monuments which were to be of immense importance to his friend Jean-François Champollion, who made a discovery in 1822: deciphering hieroglyphics. Jean Nicola Huyot made drawings of all Egypt's greatest monuments ; in some cases he was the first to have done this, in Abou Simbel or in Thebes for instance.

Next he visited Asia Minor where he made drawings of the main archaeological sites, then Greece, finally returning to Rome in 1818 where he carried out some remarkable restoration work on the ancient town around the Forums.

Once back in France in 1822, he was elected to the Academie des Beaux Arts. In 1824, Huyot, who now knew everything there was to know about Roman triumphal arches, presented plans for the completion of the Arc de l'Etoile, of which he was to become the architect and continuator until 1830.

In addition Huyot was the architect of the Palais de Justice, which he planned to renovate, although he was never able to carry out this work as he died very suddenly on 2nd August 1840. He was also one of the founder members of the Académie d'Architecture.

Guillaume Abel Blouet (1795-1853), who succeeded Huyot in July 1832 and completed work on the Arch, notably the sculpture work and inscriptions, was a descendant of Mansart. He was a Grand Prix de Rome winner and took part in this town in restoring the thermal baths of Caracalla. He went on to become a professor in the architectural section of the Ecole des Beaux-Arts. He took part in scientific exploration of Morée and published some of his drawings. He was asked to restore and extend the gardens and palace of Fontainbleau and to make them more attractive. He created in Méttray, near Tours, an "agricultural colony" for the rehabilitation of prisoners, and this was to inspire in turn many other such projects in France.

As regards the Arc de Triomphe, in addition to co-ordinating the sculpture work, a very complicated task indeed, he was also responsible for constructing the attic level, the large arched room at the top behind this attic, the upper platform and the paving around the Arch.

It was on the initiative of Blouet that the trophies which had been planned by Chalgrin on the four big façades of the pillars were replaced by four allegorical groups depicting the heroic deeds of the Republic and Empire, and that the sculptors Rude, Cortot and Etex were chosen.

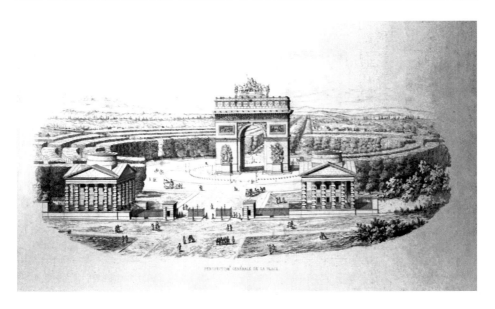

The finished Arc de Triomphe. Plans for very closely pruned hedging grown in concentric circles.

The Arch with its temporary crown as suggested by Huyot, in 1826.

A SCULPTURED MONUMENT

After a long period of uncertainty, work on the Arc de Triomphe began again in 1823 on the initiative of Louis 18th. Jean-Nicolas Huyot, a favourite of the Earl of Forbin, Minister of the Arts, and the Duke of Angoulême, son of the future Charles 10th, became Goust's assistant.

Huyot still liked the idea of projecting columns that Chalgrin had put forward in his first study. In his view, only these would give the monument the true magnificence they were seeking. Huyot had the foundations dug for these columns but the inspector general, Guy de Gisors, would not allow the work to continue. The Président du Conseil, Monsieur de Villele, dismissed the architect from office on 16th December 1825.

The architect Goust continued at the site, however, during the years 1826 and 1827, as controller of works on the arch.

A commission, made up of the architects Percier, Fontaine, Debret, Labarre and Gisors, decided in particular that the main vault should be decorated with twenty one caissons with roses between the great east and west arches and that the high relief façades should be surrounded by raised frames.

Faced with difficulties in finding big enough stones at the Château-Landon quarry, the architects turned to stone from Chérence in the region of Vexin, for the sculpture work, the large entablature, the edge arches, the projecting parts of the attic and the sculptured motifs on the large vault.

Like the stone from Château-Landon, these stones were transported to Paris by barge along the River Seine as far as the stone port on the Conférence Quay below the Cours la Reine.

In 1826 Jean-Nicholas Huyot was appointed a member of the Institute and Monsieur de Martignac, Ministre de l'Intérieur, managed to obtain his reinstatement as architect of the arch alongside Goust, on condition that he categorically respect the work already carried out. Huyot suggested certain ideas for the top of the arch which, although not accepted, did nevertheless hold work up once again.

In 1829 Huyot had a marble plaque laid into one of the foundation layers on the Paris side, which bore the following inscription :

"CE MONUMENT COMMENCÉ EN 1806 ET LONGTEMPS INTERROMPU, CONTINUÉ EN 1823 SOUS LE RÈGNE DE LOUIS XVIII, ROI DE FRANCE ET DE NAVARRE, EST CONSACRÉ À LA GLOIRE DE LOUIS ANTOINE DAUPHIN, VAINQUEUR ET PACIFICATEUR DE L'ESPAGNE. CETTE PIERRE A ÉTÉ POSÉE LE 29 JUILLET 1929.

LE VICOMTE SIMÉON, CONSEILLER D'ETAT, DIRECTEUR DES SCIENCES ET DES ARTS

LE VICOMTE HERRICART DE THURRY, CONSEILLER D'ETAT, DIRECTEUR DES TRAVAUX PUBLICS, PAR LES SOINS DE J.N. HUYOT, ARCHITECTE DU MONUMENT."

This inscription confirmed the intended purpose of the arch : to glorify the Duke of Angoulême's victories in Spain.

The architect Goust gave up his work on the site in 1830. Huyot took over ; he continued work on the entablature, put into place the keystones and the archivolts of the great arch, added a double cordon to the decoration of the small vaults around the caissons and incorporated the interlaced pattern on the double arches. He had large models built representing Charles 10th receiving the Corps d'Armées and the Duke of Angoulême receiving the municipal authorities, as well as

LE DÉPART.

sculpté par RUDE.

models of those statues that he planned to place on the top of the building. These 36 colossal statues to be placed all around the upper cornice of the monument were intended to symbolise the large towns of France. His suggestions were never taken up, Louis Philippe having already decided at his accession in July, 1830 that the Arc de Triomphe would serve its originally intended purpose : to glorify the armies of the Republic and the Empire.

showing circular medallions in high relief, the plinth of the upper cornice and balustrade, the large arched room at the top, the outer platform, and paving of the ground under and around the monument in a circle of 80 metres diameter. The whole of the interior and exterior allegorical and historical decor also remained to be done.

It was Adolphe Thiers who chose the artists for the Arc de Triomphe's decorative

The Departure of the Volunteers, details of "La Marseillaise" or "La Liberté guidant le Peuple".

On 31st July 1832 the architect Guillaume Abel Blouet was asked to replace Jean-Nicolas Huyot, dismissed from office by the inspector of Gisors for having overspent.

By this time most of the major work had been completed, since the large entablature with its cornice of lions' heads protruding two metres had been completed, as had the decoration of the vaults.

All that remained for Blouet to do was to finish off the attic level with its panels

work and he started commissioning in the summer of 1832. Those selected were Jean-Pierre Cortot, Antoine Etex, François Rude, Philippe Henri Lemaire, Bernard Gabriel Seurre, Jean-Jacques Feuchère, Jean-Emile Chaponnière, Théodore Gechter, Charles Marochetti, James Pradier, Theophile Bra, Achille Valois, Emile Seurre, Joseph de Bay, Georges Jacot and Charles-René Laitié.

The best known group is still that of François Rude which symbolises "Le Dé-

Restoration work on "La Marseillaise", in 1989.

part des Volontaires de 1792", who are carried along by the marching song of the Rhine army composed by Rouget de L'Isle and better known by the name "La Marseillaise" ever since it was sung by the federates on their way to Paris from Marseilles.

This 11.6 metre high and 6 metre wide monument shows six metre-tall figures that look as if they are emerging right out from the right hand pillar as one looks at the arch from the Champs Elysées. This is more like a sculpture in the round than a high relief even though it is not separated from the building. The same thing applies incidentally to the designs on the three other pillars.

The group of people at the base consists of, from left to right, a cavalryman in the background who is holding a horse with its head through a bridle, a foot soldier dressed in a coat of mail, wearing a Roman style helmet, holding a spear and sounding a horn ; a bare-chested man, bent over his bow which he is bracing ; in the centre the chief, richly dressed, brandishing his helmet in his left hand, ready to fight. In the foreground, a nude ephebe is wearing a helmet and holding his sword close to him ; in the background an old man appears to be giving advice to the chief who is not listening to him ; on the very right, a man wearing a helmet is drawing his sword and holding a large shield on his left arm.

Above, representing the Spirit of War, a woman is brandishing her sword to indicate the direction of the battle, her mouth wide open as she shouts. She is the famous "Marseillaise". Her furrowed brow adds to her ruggedness and she is wearing her hair in the style of the French cockerel ; behind her the wings of Victory are spread wide, the wings of a huge eagle.

The group seen on the left pillar, facing the Champs Elysées, symbolises "Le Triomphe de 1810". It was sculpted by Jean-Pierre Cortot ; its dimensions are the same as those of Rude.

The central character, more than six metres tall, is Napoleon dressed in Roman costume and holding a sword in his left hand and protecting a captured town represented by a young kneeling woman, her head bowed, with the right. To the left of the emperor, a Victory is holding an olive branch in her left hand and is placing a crown of laurel leaves on Napoleon's head.

On the left side, a seated woman, representing History, is writing on a tablet ; on the right we can see a prisoner kneeling down on one leg, his expression fierce. Above this group a winged victory is blowing a trumpet and holding a lance with the imperial eagle at the top.

"Le Triomphe de 1810" by Cortot.

LE TRIOMPHE.

sculpté par CORTOT.

The group featured on the right pillar as one looks from the Avenue de la Grande Armée represents "La Résistance de 1814". It was sculpted by Antoine Etex who has placed an upright warrior in the centre, his sword in his hand and a determined expression on his face. His left hand is holding onto a weeping woman who is carrying her dead child in her arms ; to the right the kneeling father is trying to hold her. In the background, a cavalryman is falling from his horse. At the top of the composition stands a large

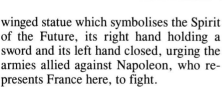

"La Résistance de 1814" by Etex.

winged statue which symbolises the Spirit of the Future, its right hand holding a sword and its left hand closed, urging the armies allied against Napoleon, who represents France here, to fight.

The group on the left pillar, on the Neuilly side, symbolises "La Paix de 1814". It too was sculpted by Antoine Etex.

In the foreground and in the centre we

LA RESISTANCE.

sculpté. par ETEX.

can see a soldier draped in a thin coat, putting his sword back into its sheath to represent the end of the war. To his left a kneeling figure, bare-shouldered, is examining a plough which symbolises a return to work in the fields. On his right a seated mother is peacefully holding her child in her lap whilst at her side a second child is busy reading. In the background, behind a peaceful warrior, is a sculpted bull standing amongst ears of corn that a labourer is trying to tie up with a piece of string. On the upper part sits enthroned an effigy of Minerva holding a spear in her left hand and leaning her right against the trunk of an olive tree.

Behind we can see an oak tree emerging on the left. A most masterfully sculpted Minerva, a crown of laurel leaves around her forehead, is shown wearing a superb Roman helmet.

O vaste entassement ciselé par l'histoire !
Monceau de pierre assis sur un monceau de gloire !
Edifice inouï !
Arc triomphal ! la foudre, en terrassant ton maître,
Semblait avoir frappé ton front encore à naître.
Par nos exploits nouveaux te voilà relevé !
Car on n'a pas voulu, dans notre illustre armée,
Qu'il fût de notre renommée
Un monument inachevé !

Dis aux siècles le nom de leur chef magnanime.
Qu'on lise sur ton front que nul laurier sublime
A des glaives français ne peut se dérober.
Lève-toi jusqu'aux cieux, portique de victoire !
Que le géant de notre gloire
Puisse passer sans se courber !

Victor Hugo, *Odes et Ballades*

Jean-Pierre CORTOT (1787-1843) was first noticed by Brideau (artist responsible for the Canonnier of the Arc du Carrousel and the high reliefs of the Colonne Vendôme, the plaster model of the elephant fountain at the Bastille, together with the architect Alavoine). Cortot sculpted with Dupaty the equestrian statue of Louis 13th, Place des Vosges, the huge pediment of the Palais Bourbon ; at the Concorde the statues of Brest and Rouen, at Père Lachaise, the high reliefs of the Casimir Périer monument.

Antoine ETEX, sculptor, painter and engraver, artist responsible for the two monuments facing the Avenue de la Grande Armée — "La Résistance de 1814" and "La Paix de 1815" — produced many works in Paris, including the statue of Sainte-Anne, on the façade of the church of Saint-Paul dans le Marais, the statue of Philippe Auguste on the left column at La Nation, the tomb of Géricault at Père Lachaise and the tomb of Raspail.

François RUDE (1794-1855) was born in Dijon. During the time of Empire, he was a pupil of Edme Gaulle who took part in building the Colonne Vendôme. "The young Rude was his assistant in this work", notes François de Saint-Simon, who has devoted a long book to the Place Vendôme and the Colonne. Rude also worked with Cartellier, who took part in the sculpture of the Arc du Carrousel, then in the restoration of the pediments at the Louvre and Invalides. He had been admitted to Louis David's workshop on the recommendation of Dominique Vivant-Denon, who saw in him an artist with a great future.

Rude prepared studies of four allegories for the Arc de Triomphe : "Le Départ", "La Retraite de Russie", "La Résistance" and "La Paix". Only one was ordered : "le Départ des Volontaires", which later became "La Marseillaise".

François Rude also sculpted the allegory "Prométhée protégeant les Arts" in Paris in 1835 on one of the walls of the Palais Bourbon as well as the recumbent statue of Godefroy-Cavaignac at the Montmartre cemetery.

LA PAIX

sculpté par ETEX.

The Funeral of Marceau

The four high reliefs on the upper part of the pillars, on either side of the main arch, are 8.3 metre long and 4 metres wide.

To the right, facing the Champs Elysées, Philippe Henri Lemaire represented in 1834 the "Funérailles de Marceau" scene.

General François Sèverin Marceau Desgravières, known as Marceau (1769-1796) was killed on 19th September 1796 near Altenkirchen in Germany when he was commander of the Sambre and Meuse army, which had taken Koblenz, Würzburg and Luxembourg.

The funeral procession is seen in front of the town walls. In the centre Marceau is laid out on a stretcher, dressed in his uniform and half draped by his own coat. Archduke Charles of Austria, bareheaded, is placing a crown on the chest of the brave general, his enemy. Behind him four Austrian officers are also paying him tribute. One soldier is gazing upon the scene and holding Marceau's horse by the bridle, whilst another is looking into the general's face. In the background to the right, an officer is in tears as he leans on a soldier who is tapping his forehead ; a young soldier is leaning on his gun.

"Les Funérailles de Marceau". High relief by Philippe Lemaire.
Drawing and detail of a soldier meditating before the body of the General.

The Battle of Aboukir

On the left, facing the Champs Elysées, Bernard Gabriel Seurre has depicted "La Bataille d'Aboukir", which took place against the Turks in Egypt, near Alexandra, on 25th July 1799.

To the left of the scene, Bonapart and Murat, followed by French soldiers, are riding on horseback towards Kinceï Mustapha, pasha of Roumelia, generalissimo of the Ottoman armies, who has just been taken prisoner by Murat.

Mustapha, very proud, is leaning against his young sons who are bowing down in respect. At the pasha's feet a prisoner is pressing his forehead into the dust, begging Bonaparte to be lenient with him. French officers can be seen behind them.

"La Bataille d'Aboukir" and the surrender of the Sultan Pasha of Roumelia. High relief by Bernard Seurre. French soldiers, the Sultan Pasha and his son, Murat on horseback, Bonaparte and Murat.

Passage du Pont d'Arcole

Facing the Avenue de la Grande Armée, on the right hand support, the high relief sculpted by Jean-Jacques Feuchère shows Bonaparte heading a detachment of foot soldiers in his "Passage du Pont d'Arcole" in Italy on 15th November 1796.

Bonaparte, with his sword in his right hand and a flag in his left, is engaging the enemy on this plank bridge, on which Colonel Muiron is lying, wounded and close to death, trying to hold the general back. Behind them able bodied officers and soldiers are advancing, others have fallen to the enemy's bullets, one of which would have killed Bonaparte had Colonel Muiron not shielded him with his own body (without this split second reaction there would have been no Empire, no carnage, no Napoleonic tyranny and, of course, no triumphal arch...) To the left of the picture Austrian batteries are firing at the group.

"Le Passage du Pont d'Arcole". High relief by Jean-Jacques Feuchère. Bonaparte, holding the red, white and blue flag, carries able-bodied and wounded soldiers.

The Capture of Alexandra

On the left hand pillar, on the Neuilly side, Jean-Emile Chaponnière has sculpted "La Prise d'Alexandrie" by Kléber on 3rd July 1798. The high relief represents General Jean-Baptiste Kléber (1753-1800, born in Strasburg and assassinated in Cairo by a muslim extremist) in front of the city walls of Alexandra. Kléber, who has been wounded, is propping his head up with his right hand and holding his sword with his left.

A grenadier is stabbing the Turk who has wounded the general with his bayonet. A nude Egyptian is making as if to hit the French soldiers whilst another Turk is trying to turn a soldier's gun away. Behind Kléber a soldier is tearing at a cartridge with his teeth and a second is trying to climb the city wall. On the opposite side the Egyptians and the Turks can be seen in the turmoil of defeat. The whole scene, as is the case throughout the whole of the Arc de Triomphe, shows astonishing realism and vigour.

"La Prise d'Alexandrie". High relief by Jean-Emile Chaponnière. (Drawing) Arab soldiers firing guns. An impassive "old soldier" reloads his gun.

*Scenes from the Battle of Alexandra,
with the wounded Kléber on the right.*

The Battle of Jemmapes

Above the small arch, on the Passy side façade in the axis of Avenue Kléber, between the keystone of the arch and the upper frieze, in a large, rectangular panel 17.3 metres long by 4 metres high, Charles Marochetti has depicted "La Bataille de Jemmapes" of 6th November 1792. This battle took place in Hainaut in Belgium with the French commanded by General Dumouriez, who captured the town occupied by the Austrians in just a few hours. Dumouriez's army included 40,000 men. The battle lasted from 7 o'clock in the morning until half past twelve midday. The battles of the Revolution and the Empire may well have been bloody, but at least they were usually quickly over !

In this high relief, Dumouriez, is riding on horseback from left to right, followed by his aides-de-camps, Bloissières, Ferrand, Rosières and Stennabosse. General Drouet has fallen from his mount and broken his leg. Closeby stands the Duke of Chartres, rallying them on by waving his hat. Dumouriez is preceded by his foot soldiers, their bayonets fitted to their rifles. To the right a group is firing at the Austrian cavalry which has just arrived on the scene. In front of the recess an Austrian officer prisoner, his head bare and his arm in a sling, appears to be wondering what fate has in store for him.

"La Bataille de Jemmapes". High relief by Charles Marochetti. Overall view of the scene, details of soldiers, horses and group of officers.

A wounded soldier protects himself from horses' hooves.
Detail of the velvet of the uniforms.

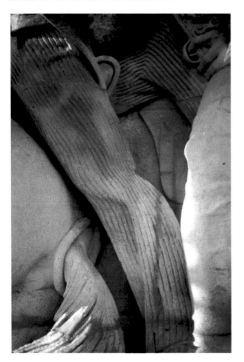

General Dumouriez accompanied by the general aides-de-camp Bloissières, Ferrand, Rosières and Steundbosse.

The Battle of Austerlitz

Above the small arch, in the axis of Avenue de Wagram, the long high relief, the same size as the one already mentioned, depicts "la Bataille d'Austerlitz", of 2nd November 1805, by Théodore Getcher. He has placed the Emporer on horseback in the centre of the composition, looking towards the enemy on the left, or his right, in other words the Russian and Austrian cavalry, whom the French are charging with their bayonnets.

General Friant has dismounted from his horse and is forcing his way through with his rifle. The sculptor has depicted the ice of Lake Sokolnitz which is breaking up under the feet of the Austrian and Russian soldiers' horses. Behind the Emporer, standing to attention in a square, with their high hats, the old guard is looking on impassively. The Emporer has stopped one guard at the front of the square with his hand. In the background, to the right, French officers on horseback, just as expressionless, are watching the scene.

On a level with or below the high relief scenes just described, can be seen four allegorical groups each with two figures,

"La Bataille d'Austerlitz". High relief by Jean François Gechter. Austrian and French infantrymen come face to face. Napoleon on horseback with the Imperial Eagle.

placed on the outer face of the arch. Two other groups are placed inside the vault, facing Avenue de Wagram and Avenue Kléber.

The small 19 metre high arches give way to the large arch (29 metres) at its transom level.

The tympanums of the arch facing the Champs Elysées are decorated with two high reliefs which portray winged renowned figures sounding a trumpet ; these graceful females sculpted by James Pradier are six metres tall. With clothing lightly draped, each is holding a crown of laurel leaves in her spare hand. They both have their hair elegantly twisted into buns as was the style of the Directory and the Empire.

The tympanums facing the Avenue de la Grande Armée also show two renowned figures sculpted by Pradier, this time holding out crowns of laurel leaves. They are facing each other, their hair tied up in buns and they are lightly veiled in very elegant drapery. The woman on the left is holding a trumpet and the one on the right a palm leaf.

The tympans of the small arch facing Avenue Kléber are decorated with allegorical characters sculpted by Achille-Joseph-Etienne Valois. On the left hand side a nude carabineer is shown from behind, his head is seen in profile, surrounded by swords, bits and buglers ; on the right hand side we can see a lancer, also nude, but this time face on, with his sabre and a rifle on the barrel of which he has placed his helmet ; spears, stirrups, epaulets and spurs complete the picture.

On the keystone is written the word CAVALERIE.

Facing Avenue Wagram the outer face, or tympans, of the arch sculpted by Théophile Bra have also been decorated with male allegorical figures : on the left is a frontal of a nude grenadier who is holding his gun and an oak branch, on the right a nude hunter is seen from behind also holding a weapon and an oak branch and to his right are a helmet, a gamebag and a sword.

On the keystone is written the word INFANTERIE.

Below the vault of the big arch, the tympans of the small arch are decorated with four other male allegories. On the Wagram-Ternes side the tympans, sculpted by Jean-Baptiste Joseph de Bay, show a frontal of a nude soldier, his foot on a cannonball, a chain wound around his left arm ; and various weapons in the background.

On the right hand side, the high relief shows depicts a young soldier, face on, holding his horse with his left hand. He symbolizes the light artillery.

On the keystone is written the word ARTILLERIE.

On the Avenue Kléber side, the tympans of the small arch under the vault of the large one were sculpted by Emile Seurre and represent two allegorical characters : on the left a cross-legged young man is seen face on placing his toe on a compass. He is leaning on nautical measuring instruments ; sails and flags can be made out in the backgound. On the right a man is seen face on holding an oak branch out in his hand in the direction of the keystone ; his other hand is resting on the branch. In the background are weapons and other objects touching on the subject of marine soldiers.

On the keystone is written the word MARINE.

The Arc de Triomphe and the Champs Elysées in 1860. A bird's eye view from a captive balloon.

Detail of the great sculpted frieze and the cornice of lions in 1988 during restoration work on the monument.

THE GREAT SCULPTED FRIEZE
THE DEPARTURE AND RETURN
OF THE ARMIES

However, the most spectacular part of the Arc de Triomphe's sculpture work, rarely matched either in France or in other parts of the world, is the frieze which goes all the way around the monument at the top of the wide, projecting patterned cornice, which itself is topped by a second frieze decorated with palm leaf shapes, from which emerge fifty rounded lions heads each over a metre tall.

The frieze goes all the way around the Arc de Triomphe building ; it covers 137 metres and is 2.12 metres high.

The scenes that are depicted, sculpted by Joseph Silvestre Brun, Georges Jacquet, Charles René Laitié and François Rude, recall "Le Départ" and "Le Retour des Armées Françaises".

"Le Départ" can be seen on the side facing the Champs Elysées and goes halfway around the other two sides. "Le Retour" can be seen facing the Avenue de la Grande Armée and on the remaining half of the other sides.

The centre of the composition in the axis of the big arch, on the Champs Elysées side, is the "Autel de la Patrie", sculpted by Sylvestre Brun, in which a symbolic flame is burning.

The procession's starting point is therefore on the left, facing Avenue Kléber.

The main figure is a winged spirit who is writing on a piece of marble the names of those who are setting out to defend their country, "La Patrie" ; followed by a cart carrying the soldiers' baggage, and a young woman in the midst of some infantry soldiers, showing a child to one of the soliders.

Facing the Champs Elysées, from left to right, the infantry procession is marching along to the sound of drums and fifes. A hussar corps, swords drawn, is galloping in front of them ; next, in order as far as "L'Autel de la Patrie", come : Chenier, Moitte, Roland, Madame Roland, Penthièvre, Marceau, Hoche, Soult, Carnot, Cambronne, Joubert, La Tour d'Auvergne, Championnet — on his knees — Jourdan, Beurnonville and La Fayette, these last three handing out flags, and finally Sieyes dressed as an abbot, the Duke of Orléans and Bailly, the first mayor of Paris, who are all facing the "Autel de la Patrie".

On the other half of the frieze we can see the Duke of Bourbon, Talleyrand, Mirabeau and Custine, with their backs to the Altar. Opposite them are General Foy, kneeling and holding a flag, Desaix, his arm outstretched, the Duke of Chartres, Masséna, Kléber, Houchard, Kellermann, Daboville, Lefevre, Augereau, Gouvion Saint-Cyr, Prince Eugène and Josephine de Beauharnais with her young daughter Hortense. Sitting in a barrow, drawing on the paper in his hand, is the painter David ; behind him the musician Gossec and Rouget de l'Isle. A little further on a soldier is stopping a cavalry corps ; next come the grenadiers playing their music and at the very end, standing still, and in a square, the "grognards de la Garde". Coming back round, on one half of the arch's north side, the Ternes-Wagram side, can be seen artillery wagons and, bringing up the rear, those of the sappers, with a winged spirit carrying a tablet.

The theme of the second half of the frieze, facing the Avenue de la Grande

CHENIER   MOITTE   ROLAND   M² ROLAND   PENTHIÈVRE   MARCEAU   HOCHE   SOULT   CARNOT   CAMBR

72

DUC DE BOURBON TALLEYRAND MIRABEAU CUSTINE FOY DESAIX DUC DE CHARTRES MASSÉNA

CHARD KELLERMANN DABOVILLE LEFEBVRE AUGEREAU GOUVION S^tCYR EUGÈNE JOSÉPHINE BEAUHARNAIS DAVID COSSEC ROUGET DE L'ISLE

Opposite : The child queen Hortense,
in the background the painter Louis David,
in the foreground Augereau
and Gouvion Saint-Cyr.
Below : Gossec and Rouget de L'Isle,
infantrymen and cavalrymen.

Cavalrymen and the Paris side of the frieze.

Baggage cart, frieze on the Passy side.

Armée and on each half of the south (Passy) and north (Ternes) façades, is *"Le Retour des Armées"*. The central part was sculpted by Louis-Denis Caillouette ; the part as one comes back round on the Passy side is the work of Bernard Gabriel Seurre ; and the part as one comes back round on the Wagram side is that of François Rude.

The central part of the composition above the keystone of the large arch is taken up by *"La France Renaissante"*, sitting on a throne.

The procession continues on the Wagram side with a figure in Egyptian dress who is drawing hieroglyphics on an obelisk to describe the exploits of the army. Next comes a wagon carrying wounded men, pulled by horses and preceded by cavalrymen. The procession continues on the large façade, with a soldier wearing a helmet on the corner and a heavy cart hauled by four oxen and loaded with a sphinx. This scene represents the return

of the Egyptian army, welcomed back by a group of men, women and children. The scene which follows shows grenadiers, cavalrymen and a figure dressed in Egyptian costume.

The procession is making its way towards the seated *"France Renaissante"*, who is holding a crown of laurel leaves in each hand and is accompanied on the right and left by two female allegories, one holding a palm leaf and the other some flowers.

The next part of the procession, going from right to left, is made up of infantrymen and cavalrymen holding flags ; next can be seen a small triumphal arch bearing the inscription : A l'Armée d'Italie, followed by a very heavy chariot hauled by four horses, one of which is falling. This chariot is pulling the statue of the Nile.

On the corner of the monument, on the Avenue Kléber side, a grognard guard is

Departing cavalrymen, frieze on the Paris side.

Moitte, Roland, Madame Roland.

Marceau, Joubert and Soult.

Soult and Carnot.

The duke of Bourbon, Talleyrand and Mirabeau.

Kellermann, Daboville and Lefevre.

The Return of the Armies, flags taken from the enemy.

The return of the Armies : cart carrying the allegorical statue of the Nile. Cart carrying wounded men.

Restoration of the Arc de Triomphe in 1989, the red, white and blue net and the "Mountaineers" carrying out cleaning work on the façades. Restoration of the Cornice of Lions.

standing quite still, watching over the transition with a last group of infantrymen in front of a chariot carrying injured men pulled by oxen, and a young woman with her child. Bringing up the rear are two horses pulling baggage and a winged Victory who is writing the conquerors'names on tablets of stone.

BATTLES AND VICTORIES

The four inside walls of the Arc de Triomphe in the direction of the large axis form wide stone pillars arranged in very regular courses.

They reach up 29 metres, as far as the Greek decoration on the first cornice level, the point at which the arches start.

On each of these four huge pillars the name of 24 major battles has been engraved, in three registers separated by crowns of laurel leaves which frame an imperial eagle or the emblem of the French cockerel, slightly raised. The names of 96 battles are written in capital letters 40 cm high.

78 other names are written on the inside and outside of the monument, on the pillars of the small arches, as well as to the left and right of the four big high reliefs underneath the small arch vault.

The names of the war heroes of the First Republic and of the Empire are written in four huge lists, each divided into ten columns or vertical registers. These lists have been placed in the centre of the four outer faces of the small arches. Above them are four high reliefs. In all six hundred and sixty names are included in these lists.

On the west side, on the inner façace of the west pillar, on the Avenue Kléber side, can be seen the names of marshals, generals, army officers of the eastern Pyrenees and the western Pyrenees, armies of the west, reserve armies, Boulogne camp and the Great Army.

The high relief above this, 8 metres long and 2.50 metres tall, was sculpted by Jean-Joseph Espercieux. Its theme is *"La Victoire de l'Ouest"*, portrayed as a figure sitting in the centre, wings outstretched, holding large laurel branches over the heads of 4 Spirits. Two of these are carrying a garland of flowers and fruit ; the one on the left is holding out a broken sceptre ; behind him, in a cartridge, are written the names Jemmapes and Fleurus. The spirit on the right is holding out a broken diadem ; at their feet lay helmets and vases. To the left and the right of this high relief the words : "TOULOUSE — M DEL RIOSERO — OPORTO — FUNTO D'OMORO — ROSES — ASTORGA — GIRONE and OLIVENZA are engraved.

The names which have been engraved on the south side are those of the war heroes who fought at Dalmatia, in Egypt, Spain, Andalucia, Aragon, Catalonia and Portugal. The high relief, measuring 8 metres by 2.52, was sculpted by Antoine François Gérard. In the centre "La Victoire du Sud" is sitting with wings outstretched. She is holding a sceptre bearing the imperial eagle in her right hand and in her left a tablet on which are written the names Marengo, Rivoli, Arcole and Lodi. On the left two spirits are forming a trophy with their weapons, helmets and armour. On the right a spirit is holding a palm leaf and is placing a crown on Napoleon's head, set upon a pedestal, which another spirit is sculpting. On the pedestal is the imperial eagle wearing a crown.

To the left and right of the high relief of the *"Victoire du Sud"* are written the words : "ADIGE - MONTAGNE NOIRE - POZZOLA - LA PIAVE - NAPLES - PLAISANCE - MADRID - MEQUINENZA".

On the east side the heroes'names are those of the armies of the Danube, Helvetica, the Alpine Grisons, the Var, Italy, Rome and Naples. *"La Victoire de l'Est"*

ALMY JEMMAPES FLEURUS MORENOË LODI CORDONE ARCOLE RIVOLI PYRAMIDES ABOUKIR

KOMAER ZURICH HELIOPOLIS MARENGO HOHENLINDEN ULM AUSTERLITZ IENA FRIEDLAND SIERRA

SLING, WAGRAM MOSCOWA LUTZEN BAUTZEN DRESDE HANAU MORMANT MONTEREAU LIGNY

LILLE	WERTINGEN	LOANO	LE BASTAN
HONDSCHOOTTE	GUNTZBOURG	MILLESIMO	LE BOULOU
WATTIGNIES	ELCHINGEN	DEGO	BURGOS
ARLON	DIERNSTEIN	MONDOVI	ESPINOSA
COURTRAI	HOLLABRUNN	ROVEREDO	TUDELA
TOURCOING	SAALFELD	BASSANO	UCLEZ
WEISSEMBOURG	HALLE	S.˭ GEORGES	LA COROGNE

MAESTRICHT	PRENTZLOW	MANTOUE	SARRAGOSSE
ALDENHOVEN	LUBECK	TAGLIAMENTO	VALLS
LANDAU	PULTUSK	SEDIMAN	MEDELIN
NEUWIED	EYLAU	MONT THABOR	MARIA-BELCHITE
RASTADT	OSTROLENKA	CHEBREISSE	ALMONACID
ETLINGEN	DANTZIG	BASSIGNANO	OCANA
NERESHEIM	HEILSBERG	SAN GIULIANO	ALBA DE TORMÈS
BAMBERG	LANDSHUT	DIETIKON	VIQUE
AMBERG	ECKMULH	MUTTA THAL	LERIDA
FRIEDBERG	RATISBONNE	GENES	CIUDAD-RODRIGO

BIBERACH	RAAB	LE VAR	ALMEIDA
ALTENKIRCHEN	MOHILEW	MONTEBELLO	TORTOSE
SCHLIENGEN	SMOLENSKO	LE MINCIO	GEBORA
KEHL	VALONTINA	CALDIERO	BADAJOZ
ENGEN	POLOTSK	CASTEL FRANCO	TARRAGONE
MOESKIRCH	KRASNOË	RAGUSE	SAGONTE
HOCHSTETT	WURSCHEN	GAETE	VALENCE

is an 8 metre by 2.30 metre high relief, sculpted by Joseph Adolphe Alexandre Walcher.

The Victory is sitting on a garland, her feet upon on a crocodile and she is holding a tablet under her left arm inscribed with the names of the Battles of Alexandra, the Pyramids, Aboukir and Heliopolis. On the right are two spirits, each holding out a hand to the other ; the end one is crowning the other. All around them are canons, spears and shields. On the left, one of the spirits is planting a flag into the ground whilst the other is trying to pull it out. The names "JAFFA - PESCHIERA - LE CAIRE - CAPRÉE - GRATZ - C. DE SPRIMONT - GEISBERG - CHAMPAUBERT".

On the north side can be seen the high relief *"La Victoire du Nord"*, sculpted by Astyanax Bosio. She is sitting, wings outstretched, and surrounded by weapons. In her left hand she is holding a tablet bearing the names of the victories which took place at Austerlitz, Iena, Friedland, Ulm, Wagram and Eylau. With her right hand she is pointing to a crown with a small dagger. On the right and left spirits are holding palm leaves, garlands and drums, and various weapons can be seen around them. On each side of the high relief, to the left and right, are written the names : "DIERSHEIM - DUSSELDORF - GRAND-PORT - MALO JOROSLAWIETZ - YPRES - LUXEMBOURG - BRESLAW - BERG - OP ZOUM".

The names engraved on the panels of this pillar are those of the heroes who won fame in the armies of the North Ardennes, the Moselle, the Rhine, Sambre and Meuse, the Rhine and Moselle, Holland and Hanover.

Over the very wide, projecting cornice above the long, sculpted frieze telling of *"Le Départ"* and *"Le Retour des Armées"*, is a very big attic level, built in proportion to the monument. This attic is 7.25 metres high. Thirty six very wide pilasters, each one decorated with a sword laid upon palm leaves and with the point facing up, separate this attic into square panels.

On these panels can be seen round, convex shields, each surrounded by a garland of oak leaves. The names of the Republic and the Empire's major victories are engraved on them, namely :

— facing the Champs Elysées, from left to right : "VALMY - JEMMAPES - FLEURUS - MONTENOTTE - LODI - CASTIGLIONE - ARCOLE - RIVOLI - LES PYRAMIDES - ABOUKIR - ALKMAER",

— facing the Avenue de la Grande Armée, from left to right : "ULM - AUSTERLITZ - IÉNA - FRIEDLAND - SOMO-SIERRA - ESSLING - WAGRAM - LA MOSKOVA-LUTZEN - BLEUTZEN - DRESDE",

— facing avenue de Wagram : "ZURICH - HELIOPOLIS - MARENGO - HOHENLIDEN",

— facing avenue Kléber : "HANAU - MONTMIRAIL - MONTEREAU - LAGNY".

The gallery at the very top of the arch is formed from an elegant, continuous balustrade, made up of thirty six large Medusa heads separated by an interval of three antique style shields. On the side façades of the attic, an opening placed in the centre allows light to enter the rooms on the upper level.

The three vaults of the Arc de Triomphe — the main vault consisting of three registers each with eight caissons, and the side vaults consisting of five registers each with ten caissons — are decorated with high relief sculpted roses, modelled on acanthus flowers in full bloom. The sculpted shapes of laurel branches separate the caissons ; around the central acanthus runs a double row of ova and palm leaves.

The caissons of the large vault.

HEROES OF THE ARC DE TRIOMPHE

In his writings about the Place de l'Etoile, François de Saint-Simon tells how in 1835, when the arch was nearing completion, the architect Blouet was struck by how bear the walls were, in particular those of the small arches. He came up with the idea of engraving the names of the battles and heroes of the Republic and Empire on the large stone panels which had been left free. He sent a proposal to Adolphe Thiers, Minister of the Interior at the time, to this effect. The minister thought it an excellent idea and gave his full approval to the project.

Lieutenant General, Baron of Saint-Cyr Nugues, was given the task of drawing up a list with the names of the officers and battles to be commemorated. The space available on the four inside walls of the small arches, consisting of six columns, each with sixteen names meant that three hundred and eighty four names could be placed in alphabetical order in vertical tables, but also in geographical order of south, north, east or west, according to the European region in which each officer had made his name.

No sooner had the arch been inaugurated on 29th July 1836 than protests began over the scandalous omission of forgotten names....

Space was limited, yet many survivors of the imperial armies or their families felt that they too had a right to such glorification, all the more so since the first name to figure on the east panel, in the fourth column, was that of Turreau, the "butcher" of the Vendée who, whilst heading the fiendish troops of the Convention, had carried out what can only be described as a veritable genocide in this department [1].

The name of General Hugo, who had taken part in the dreadful Spanish campaigns, was not mentioned either, although Victor Hugo made no protest, other than through his two famous verses in Les Voix Intérieures, of 1837 : "I have no regrets before this sublime wall — But for absent Phidias [2] and my forgotten father".

Louis Philipp's government decided to calm matters by adding the forgotten names to further tables. Amongst these figured such prestigious names as Kellermann, Desaix, Lepic, Ordener and Moreau... ! and even Louis Bonaparte, whose name was later engraved under the statue of the "Victoire du Sud", just above that of Colonel Chabert.

In 1834, Marshal Soult, Duke of Dalmatia, President of the Council and Minister of War at the time, gave the architect Blouet the job of finding a solution !

A commission, presided over by Marshal Oudinot, Duke of Reggio, Grand Chancelier de la Légion d'Honneur at the time, was put in charge of looking into all claims and ascertaining the names of those general officers considered worthy of inclusion on the Arch, in an attempt to avoid any further objections later on.

The commission suggested 233 new names of generals and 70 names of battles to Marshal Soult. However, the architect could only find space for 128 on a series of side panels. The Minister of Public Works, Mr. Teste, was of the opinion that the marshal was asking for too many names to be included. By way of reply Soult wrote a letter to the Minister on 31st March 1841 saying :

"Far from consenting to the withdrawal of a single name from the list drawn up by the Commission I would, on the contrary, be prepared to add further ones which have been overlooked. The objection that

---

1. It was not until 1985 that the writer and historian Michel Ragon assessed this genocide in his work *Les Mouchoirs rouges de Cholet*.

2. Hugo proved to be particularly severe with the sculptors of the Arc de Triomphe, who did not deserve such censure, regretting the absence of such talent as that of Phidias, responsible for the Parthenon frieze in Athens in the 5th century BC.

it will not be possible to write names on the sides of the monument does not, in my view, constitue a real difficulty, even if a harmonious imbalance should result ; I would rather this than any oversight... I would even add that this singularity would, in my opinion, show very good taste since the illustrious names would contribute more to the monument's splen-

dour than could the most outstanding architectural embellishments. Given these considerations, I would ask you to kindly accept my insistance that all the names under discussion be engraved on the Arc de Triomphe, otherwise it may be necessary to exclude them all ; but I like to think that it will not come to such a measure. "

Blouet therefore decided to have 16 ex-

Restoration of the vault in 1988 under the direction of the architect Michel Marot.

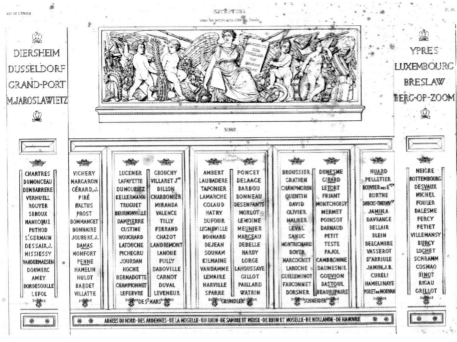

ARC DE L'ÉTOILE

INSCRIPTIONS
sous les petits arcs côté du Nord

Pl. 16

DIERSHEIM
DUSSELDORF
GRAND-PORT
M.JAROSLAWIETZ

NORD

YPRES
LUXEMBOURG
BRESLAW
BERG-OP-ZOOM

CHARTRES	VICHERY	LUCKNER	GROUCHY	AMBERT	PONCET	BROUSSIER	DUHESME	HUARD	NEIGRE
DUMONCEAU	MARGARON	LAFAYETTE	VILLARET J	LAUBADERE	DELAAGE	GRATIEN	GIRARD	PELLETIER	ROTTEMBOURG
DEMBARRERE	GÉRARD,J.	DUMOURIEZ	DILLON	TAPONIER	BARBOU	CHAMPMORIN	LETORT	BOMER dit E^{TTE}	DESVAUX
VERHUELL	PIRÉ	KELLERMANN	CHARBONIER	LAMARCHE	BONNEAU	QUENTIN	FRIANT	BURTHE	MICHEL
ROUYER	BALTUS	TRUGUET	MIRANDA	COLAUD	DESENFANTS	DAVID	MONTCHOISY	DECS-THOMY	FOULER
SEROUX	PROST	BEURNONVILLE	VALENCE	HATRY	MORLOT	OLIVIER	MERMET	JAMINA	DALESME
MANICQUE	DOMHANGET	DAMPIERRE	TILLY	DUFOUR	LEMOINE	MALHER	POINSOT	DAVRANCE	PERCY
PUTHOD	BONNAIRE	CUSTINE	FERRAND	LIGNEVILLE	MEUNIER	LEVAL	DARNAUD	BELLAIR	PETIET
S^t.GERMAIN	JOUBERT,J.	HOUCHARD	CHAZOT	BONNARD	MARCEAU	SAHUC	PETIT	BLEIN	VILLEMANSY
DESSAIX,J.	DAMAS	LATOUCHE	LANDREMONT	DEJEAN	DEBELLE	MONTRICHARD	TESTE	DELCAMBRE	BURCY
MISSIESSY	HONFORT	PICHEGRU	LANOUE	SOUHAM	HARDY	BOYER	PAJOL	VASSEROT	LOCHET
VANDERMAESEN	PENNE	JOURDAN	FULLY	KILMAINE	LORGE	MARCOGNET	CAMBRONNE	D'ARRIULE	SCHRAMM
DOUMERC	HAMELIN	HOCHE	DABOVILLE	VANDAMME	LAHOUSSAYE	LABOCHE	DAUMESNIL	JAMIN,J.B.	COSMAO
AMEY	HULOT	BERNADOTTE	CARNOT	LEMAIRE	GILLOT	GUILLEMINOT	GOUVION	CURELI	BINOT
BORDESOULLE	BABDET	CHAMPIONNET	DUVAL	HARVILLE	PAILLARD	FAUCONNET	BASTOUL	HAMELINAYE	RIGAU
LEFOL	VILLATTE	LEFEBVRE	LEVENEUR	SPARRE	WATRIN	DORSNER	BEAUREPAIRE	PORET de MORVAN	GRILLOT

DE St MARS — GRUNDLER — SCHNEIDER

ARMEES DU NORD · DES ARDENNES · DE LA MOSELLE · DU RHIN · DE SAMBRE ET MEUSE · DE RHIN ET MOSELLE · DE HOLLANDE · DE HANOVRE

INSCRIPTIONS
sous les petits arcs côté du Sud

JAFFA
PESCHIERA
CAIRE
CAPRÉE

EST

GRATZ
C.DE SPRIMONT
GEISBERG
CHAMPAUBERT

NARBONNE	BOYELDIEU	MOREAU	GERARD	TURREAU	DESJARDINS	CARA S^t CYR	BEAUPUY	BARBANÈGRE	AUBRY
CLARKE	BERCKHEIM	BRUIX	MAISON	DESSOLES	MANSOUTY	DECOUZ	VALHUBERT	DUPRAT	ROUSSEL D'H^t
THARREAU	ORNANO	MICHAUD	MOUTON	BONET	DELMAS	CURIAL	DEBILLY	MARIN	LEPIC
LEMAROIS	KNIAZIEWICZ	GOUMON S^t CYR	LECOURBE	COMPANS	FURION	BEAUMONT	CAMPANA	GAUTHERIN	L'HERITIER
TREILLARD	PLAUSONNE	NEY	Ste SUZANNE	MONTBRUN	CLAPAREDE	CERVONI	GAUTIER	PELET	JACQUINOT
DUTAILLIS	DERY	MACDONALD	FERINO	LARIBOISSIERE	BISSON	LT MAUBOURG	CAULAINCOURT	PELLEPORT	BOURCKE
FOUCHER	CHOUARD	OUDINOT	GRENIER	GUDIN	WALTHER	LASALLE	LACUÉE	MONTMARIE	DOMON
CLÉMENT,L.R.	BOYER,J	DAVOUST	SCHAL	MORAND	BRUYERE	DURUTTE	HICONET	CAMPI	GIRARDIN
DELAGRANGE,A.	GOURÉ	LANNES	BOURCIER	LEGRAND	BOUDET	KLEIN	MORLAND	DURRIEU	DARU
MARULAZ	SÉCUR,PH.	MORTIER	RICHEPANSE	LABOISSIERE	ROCHAMBEAU	HEUDELET	MAZAS	WATHIEZ	COÉHORN
GUYOT de LACOUR	VALLIN	BESSIERES	ÉBLÉ	CHERIN	DELZONS	DONZELOT	VIALA	SCHRAMM,J.	ROUSSEL
DEFRANCE	LALAING D'AUD	PONIATOWSKI	MARESCOT	SORBIER	COMROUX	BELLAVESNE	H^{te} LAHOTTE	VINCENT	GIRARD dem VIEUX
DUMOUSTIER	DELAGRANGE,CH.	ROSILY	RAPP	KIRGENER	D'HAUTPOUL	TEULIÉ	MARION	GENTILS'ALP	GUYOT
ALMÉRAS	MONTESQUIOU-F^{ZX}	LAURISTON	SAVARY	DUROC	DESPAGNE	FRESSINET	HERVO	FOISSAC-LAT	DAHLMANN
ALBERT	DEDON	VILLENEUVE	DROUET	M^{le} DUMAS	CORBINEAU	DÉMONT	CHAMBURE	LAMARÈRE	BRUN
CHEMINEAU	WATHIER	MOLITOR	BERTRAND	SONGIS	GRANJEAN	ABATTUCCI	LT D'AUVERGNE	LEJEUNE	ROMEUF

MOREAUX — GROS — ROSAMEL

ARMEES DU DANUBE · D'HELVETIE · DES GRISONS · DES ALPES · DU VAR · D'ITALIE · DE ROME · DE NAPLES

Martin ainé scrip.

INSCRIPTIONS
sous les petits arcs, côté de Passy

ADIGE									NAPLES
MONTAGNE NOIRE									PLAISANCE
POZZOLO									MADRID
LA PIAVE									MEQUINENZA

SUD

KELLERMANN,F	RUTY	ANSELME	SERURIER	BON	CHARPENTIER	POUGET	GRIGNY	MAGON	BACHELU
RIVAUD de la Rre	SOULT,P.	BRUNET	MURAT	LANUSSE	DAMAS	LASALCETTE	CHAMPEAUX	PONTEVIN de Mr	MEUNIER,C.
FIORELLA	DIGEON	BIRON	BEAUHARNAIS	RUSCA	GAZAN	SOULÈS	CHARTON	BESSIÈRES,B.	BRICHE
VIGNOLLE	LAPLANE	DUMERBION	MARMONT	CARDANNE	BEKER	CAMPREDON	BAYRAND	CAVAIGNAC	THOUVENOT
FAULTRIER	JEANIN	MONTESQUIOU	MENOU	DUBOIS	MARCHAND	CHABRAN	POINT	GUDIN,P.	MERLIN
CAFFARELLI,A.	DODE	DUMAS	PERRÉE	St HILAIRE	DALLEMAGNE	VIAL	BOISGERARD	DELAITRE	DEJEAN,A.
SANSON	FABRE	MASSENA	LAPOYPE	GARNIER	CHABERT	BERTHEZENE	DUPHOT	BORZELLI	SUBERVIE
PERNETY	DELAMOTTE,A	BERTHIER	REYNIER	DOMBROWSKY	COLLI	EXCELMANS	BANEL	MONTÉLÉGIER	BIGARRÉ
LASOWSKI	GARBÉ	AUGEREAU	LAHARPE	DOMMARTIN	ZAYONSCHECK	LEDRU des ESs	STENGEL	BERGE	LARREY
SARRUT	STROLTZ	JOUBERT	RAMPON	VERDIER	PARTOUNEAUX	DARRICAU	VALLONGUE	MERLIN,E.	LAMETH,CH.
ARRIGHI	QUIOT	KLEBER	BELLIARD	MENARD	DUPAS	CASSAGNE	SULKOSKY	VALAZÉ	CAUSSE
DANTHOUARD	RÉMOND,V.	BRUEYS	ANDREOSSY	FRERE	ROGUET	CAFFARELLI	LETURC	LUCOTTE	LAHURE
EMERIAU	BONNEMAINS	DESAIX	CHASSELOUP?	MIOLLIS	MONIER	DELEGORGUES	MIREUR	LOVERDO	ROIZE
RAZOUT	St GENIÉS	BRUNE	GUYEUX	DUGUA	RICARD	RAMBAUD	DESNOYERS	BAUROT	HARISY
DÉRIOT	WILLAUMEZ	SCHAWEMBOURG	VAUBOIS	SERAS	MAIMONI	CACAULT	MARIGNY	LACOMB-DIAMIAC	HORANGIES
*TIRLET	LAMORANDIÈRE	CANTHEAUME	Bt DHILLIERS	DESTAING	PARTHOD	PIJON	BLANCHEVILLE	DESCENETTES	BRON
		CHAMORIN		DENNIÉE		S:LAURENT			

ARMÉES DE DALMATIE · D'ÉGYPTE · D'ESPAGNE · DE PORTUGAL · D'ANDALOUSIE · D'ARAGON · DE CATALOGNE · DU MIDI

INSCRIPTIONS
sous les petits arcs côté de Chaigny

ROSES									TOULOUSE
ASTORGA									M.del RIOSECO
GIRONE									OPORTO
OLIVENZA									FUENTE d'OUORO

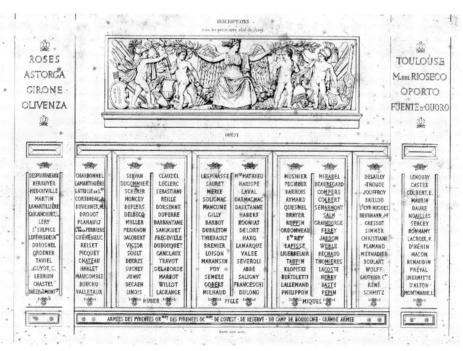

OUEST

DESFOURNEAUX	CHARBONNEL	SERVAN	CLAUZEL	LESPINASSE	Mt MATHIEU	MUSNIER	MIRABEL	DESAILLY	LENOURY
BERRUYER	LAMARTINIÈRE	DUCOMMIER	LECLERC	SAURET	HARISPE	PECHEUX	BEAUREGARD	TROUDE	CASTEX
HEDOUVILLE	LATULLE de Lt	SCHERER	SEBASTIANI	MERLE	LAVAL	BARROIS	COMPERE	JOUFFROY	COLBERT,E.
MARTIN	CORBINEAU	MONCEY	REILLE	SOLIGNAC	DARMAGNAC	AYMARD	COLBERT	BAILLOD	MAURIN
LAMARTILLIÈRE	DUVERNET,M	DEFLERS	DORSENNE	MANCUNE	DAULTANNE	QUESNEL	SEMARMONT	St CYR HUGUES	DAURE
CAULAINCOURT,A	DROUOT	DELBECQ	DUPERRE	GILLY	HABERT	BRAYER	SALM	BEURMANN,F	NOAILLES
LERY	FLANAULT	MULLER	BARBANTANE	BARBOT	ROGNIAT	RUFFIN	GRAINDORGE	CRESSOT	SERCEY
St SULPICE	Ct LA FERRIERE	PERIGNON	SAHUGUET	DUBRETON	DELORT	ORDONNEAU	FEREY	SIMMER	BONNAMY
LEFÉVRESDESN	GUÉHÉNEUC	DAGOBERT	FRECEVILLE	THIEBAULT	HAXO	Et REY	JARDON	CHRISTIANI	LACROIX,P.
DUROSNEL	REISET	VICTOR	DUBOUQUET	BRENIER	LAMARQUE	LAPISSE	WEBLE	FLAMAND	D'HÉNIN
ORDENER	PICQUET	DEGRES	CANCLAUX	LOISON	VALEE	LIGERBELAIR	BECHAUD	MEYNADIER	MACON
TAVIEL	CHATEAU	SUCHET	TRAVOT	MARANSIN	SEVEROLI	TAUPIN	THOMIERES	BOULART	RENAUDIN
GUYOT,C.	HARLET	JUNOT	DELABORDE	POY	ABBÉ	KLOPISKI	LACOSTE	WOLFF	PRÉVAL
LEBRUN	MAUCOMBLE	DECAEN	MARBOT	SEMELE	SALIGNY	BERTOLETTI	HENRY	GAUTHIER,Ct	LHERMITTE
CHASTEL	BOUCHU	LINOIS	WILLOT	GOBERT	FRANCESCHI	LALLEMAND	BASTE	RENÉ	D'ALTON
BAILLY de MONT	VALLETAUX		LAGRANGE	MILHAUD	DULONG	PHILIPPON	PEPIN	SCHMITZ	MONTMARIE,L
		HUBER		PILLE		MIQUEL			

ARMÉES DES PYRÉNÉES OR.tes DES PYRÉNÉES OC.tes DE L'OUEST · DE RÉSERVE · DU CAMP DE BOULOGNE · GRANDE ARMÉE

Marié ainé sculp.

tra panels engraved on the side supports of the small arches. In the meantime 7 more names had been added to the marshal's list. In 1842 the marshal asked for a further 12 new names to be added. The architect had to find room for them in the centre tables, at the base of the columns between the Croix d'Honneur.

Still Louis and Jérôme Bonaparte had been forgotten ! This omission only came to light in 1850, once Louis Napoléon was president of the Republic ! Their names were added, one under *"La Victoire du Sud"* and the other on *"La Victoire du Nord"*. So it was that by 1850 there were 654 names. A further six requests were made and accepted in 1851, 1893 and 1895. This meant there were now 700 names in all, but still the name of General Hugo was not included. As for the famous battles and victories, these had now reached 174 in number.

CROWNS
FOR THE ARCH

Although no crown was ever finally built on the Arc de Triomphe, many plans were drawn up with this in mind.

In 1826 a commission of four architects — Debret, de Gisors, Fontaine and Labarre — agreed that a number of different figures and cavaliers depicting "Europe at peace, free France and the Arts and Literature leading to Abundance" ought to be added.

Their proposal was not accepted and neither was that of the architect Médous who, in 1830, came up with the idea of a huge dome crowned with a star and decorated with a globe.

As for Chauvin, he was thinking more along the lines of an enormous royal crown. Huyot designed an imperial chariot pulled by eight horses ; Rude, an ancient cavalier and various figures for the frieze ; Farcy a gigantic eagle, a sphinx and a lion ; an unknown artist : *"La Paix sur le globe terrestre environne les Arts"* ; the sculptor Pradier, in 1832, reverted to the idea of an imperial eagle placed on a stack of arms and flags, with Napoleon in coronation dress.

In 1838 the sculptor Seurre, who had helped to decorate the arch in previous years, designed a crown showing "Triumphal France on a chariot pulled by six horses" ; in the corners were characters symbolizing the points of the compass.

As for the architect Blouet, he favoured a monument to the French Armies showing France dressed in a toga ruling over eagles and with renowned figures on winged horses. An alternative version replaced Napoleon with France. Antoine Etex, who had also contributed to the sculpture work of the arch, put forward ideas for two different versions of a chariot drawn by six horses ; Antoine Devéria, two versions of the emperor, one being carried by an eagle and the other by a horse, with allegories of the Victory.

Not did plans stop there...

In 1852 the sculptor Antoine Barye constructed a model of an eagle perched with outstretched wings on a globe, a bronze version of which is now kept in the Louvre Museum ; he sought permission from the Minister of Fine Arts to present his study to Prince Louis Napoleon, soon to become Emperor Napoleon 3rd.

In 1853 the sculptor Barre exhibited a much more ambitious project. This showed Napoleon on horseback, holding the sceptre of Charlemagne in a chariot pulled by a team of four horses galloping along at full speed. On the corners of the monument the four kings (Joseph, King of Naples and Spain, Jerome, King of Westphalia, Murat, King of Naples and Louis, King of Holland) can be seen on their horses. In the square around the arch are twelve statues of famous people enthroned on pedestals.

David d'Angers came up with the idea of a statue of Liberty towering over Paris.

Plans of a crown by Blouet (1832-1836), below ; by Chauvin (1834), right ; by Médous (1830), left.

In 1858, Elias Robert, a pupil of David d'Angers, presented Napoleon on a globe, dressed in coronation clothes, and accompanied by renowned figures on horseback. For twenty years or so imaginations died down, and indeed no work on any of the projects already described was ever started.

In 1887 Alexandre Falguière sculpted a model of a crown based on the theme of the Republic's triumphs. This large-scale model, made in plaster, was placed on top of the building. It stayed there from 1881 to 1886 before being destroyed, cast bronze being judged too costly.

Falguière's study, which figures in numerous photographs and engravings of the period, shows a quadriga, with the figure of the Republic sitting in the centre and two young women holding the horses by the bridle. It is certainly lacking neither in lyricism nor in grandeur.

Whilst carrying out restoration work on the arch in 1988-1989, Michel Marot, winner of the Grand Prix of Rome, Chief Architect of Civil Buildings and National Palaces and a professor at the Ecole des Beaux-Arts, also put forward his ideas for a project. His plan was to construct, with simple steel tubes, a 50 centimetre mesh around a map of France highlighted by a central space and positioned at such an angle as to be easily seen from either side. At night special lighting effects would cast a red, white and blue beam of light. The tubular construction, with a less rigid exterior outline, symbolized Liberty ; the two harmonious forms, the floating lightness of the structure and the central emptiness expressed a dialogue of Fraternity ; Equality was symbolized by the construction's harmony.

Plans of a crown by the architect Michel Marot, in 1989: silhouette of France in three colours.

Plans of a crown by Alexandre Falguière, made in 1886. Model of the quadriga pulling the chariot of Peace. The quadriga on top of the Arch in 1890.

THE PLACE DE L'ETOILE AFTER COMPLETION OF THE ARC DE TRIOMPHE

Having placed the Grand Cours between the Palais des Tuileries and Chaillot Hill in 1676-1675, Le Nôtre had planned to incorporate a circus at the top of the hill to finish the whole perspective off in a befitting way. He designed a regular shaped octagon from which branched out, in addition to the Champs Elysées and Avenue de Neuilly, six other roads leading to Ternes, Passy, Chaillot, the Bois de Boulogne, Boulogne and Saint-Cloud.

The Parisien lawyer Barbier, editor of a newspaper at the beginning of the 18th century, noted in 1720 : *"it had been the fashion that year to go to the Etoile to see the Bezons fair returning"*. The memorialist was talking about the famous fair held every August in Ternes, near the main Paris highway at Garennes-Bezons, also known as the Bezons road, by the old Neuilly bridge. The fairground roundabouts and stalls were set up on the ground along which Avenue Mac Mahon now runs.

In the last third of the 18th century, at the end of Louis 15th's reign, Le Nôtre, who had hitherto limited his plans to stopping at the village of Neuilly, began to set his sights further afield, as far as the circus at Chante-Coq at Courbevoie (later to become the Défense circus), with the construction of Neuilly bridge, built by the engineer Jean-Rodolphe Perronet, and first put into service in 1772.

This building work had the effect of lowering the height of the Etoile de Chaillot Hill, near to which the Marquis of Marigny, Director of Buildings, had a public garden planted out. Entertainments and open-air cafes sprang up. This walkway was called the "Promenoir de Chaillot" ; it ceased to exist in 1860.

In 1800, on his return from exile in England, Chateaubriand wrote :

"It was a Sunday and we were returning to Paris by way of the Etoile Gate. To my amazement I heard the sound of violins, clarinets and drums ; I caught sight of men and women dancing to a band".

At the beginning of Louis 16th's reign, after 1774, work continued on levelling out the ground at the Etoile circus, the average height of which has been reduced by four or five metres. The resulting earth was taken away to the Paris side, to the right of the Champs Elysées, resulting in the artificial hillock down which Rues Washingdon, Balzac, Arsène Houssaye and Lord Byron now run.

In 1784 the "Fermiers Généraux" were given permission by the Minister Charles Alexandre de Calonne, General Controller of Finances, to have a wall built all the way around Paris into which were set sixty toll gates, twenty four of which were main entrances, thus enabling a stricter control on products being transported into the capital and tolls to be levied which would plenish the coffers of the Town and of the State.

This huge, 23 kilometre long fence marked out the perimeter of Paris (3370 hectares) until 1860, and was erected in just a few years by the architect Claude Nicolas Ledoux. At the end of the Champs Elysées, Ledoux built two magnificent city tollhouses. These buildings were crowned by low circular towers with triangular pediments on each façade. A gate that allowed pedestrians and carriages to pass through linked them. They were not demolished until 1860 when Haussmann extended the perimeter of the town as far as

1. Stretching over a distance of 42 kilometres and 600 to 800 metres wide, the fortifications of Paris were the biggest after the Great Wall of China ; it enclosed an area of 7,802 hectares.

The Arch and square in 1866, painting by Louis Ricois.

On the Champs Elysées, the country-side was close to us : as soon as you had passed the Etoile gate, small pieces of cultivated land on the Avenue de Saint-Cloud and the Ternes appeared meaning that the fields were not far off ; in the gardens the scent of lilac, violets, yellow stocks and wisteria hung heavy in the air. When you reached Porte Maillot you felt like you were off on a journey.

Countess of Armaillé, *Mémoires.*

the fortified wall built at the end of Louis Philippe's reign.

In 1786 the Knight of Poulet opened up a big building close to the Etoile walkway, intended as a military orphenage school. This philantropical institution, which received the support of Louis 16th, was closed down during the time of the Revolution, when the Knight of Poulet was despoiled by the nation. The buildings quickly fell into ruin.

A hippodrome was built in its place during the reign of Louis Philippe and it was here that the Franconis gave their horse shows which met with so much success that they had to call upon the help of horsewomen, as pretty as they were famous, such as the legendary Céleste Mogador. At this time hippodromes were big covered circuses. The Etoile hippodrome was built under a wooden frame. It could house 15,000 spectators. From the side of the Arc de Triomphe, opposite the square, it could not be missed with its monumental Moor style entrance.

In May 1848, following the revolutionary riots, the "Fête de la Fraternité" was celebrated there. Aeronauts took off in their strange balloons, such as the first airship designed by Giffard in 1852. In 1855, the hippodrome was demolished to allow for permanent improvements to be made to the Place de l'Etoile by Haussmann and Hittorff. It was moved to near the Avenue Saint-Cloud circus (Place Victor Hugo).

Even though the Arc de Triomphe was finished in 1836, the Place de l'Etoile still retained a rather chaotic and messy look for another fifteen years, with a large embankment on the Ternes side, and mounds on the Chaillot side, the highest point being within the triangle formed by what are now Avenue Kléber and Avenue Victor Hugo.

In 1853, Napoleon 3rd decided that the Etoile should be redeveloped and Haussmann entrusted this work to Jacques Ignace Hittorff. The Emporer approved the project on 13th August 1854. The architect designed a circular area 240 metres in diameter. The Avenue du Bois, 1,300 metres long and 120 wide, was now nearing completion. Haussmann went on to have the Bois de Boulogne replanted and completely transformed. The Prefect wanted to extend the Bois de Boulogne as far as Paris by creating a grandiose avenue leading from the Etoile — 120 metres wide as opposed to 70 — wider than the Champs Elysées, adorned with huge planted gardens. Hittorff had to reduce it in size towards the Place de l'Etoile end in order to make it the same width as the other main roads : widening the Avenue de l'Impératrice (Avenue du Bois until 1929, Avenue Foch since) gave this an extraordinary sense of openess.

In 1854 work began on levelling out the ground around the Arc de Triomphe once and for all. The old Champs Elysées tollhouses were eventually demolished in 1860.

A circular road — Rue de Tilsitt and Rue de Presbourg — ran around the square behind the twelve majestic private hotels erected by Hittorff. Each building, the beauty of its façade enhanced by its grand Corinthian pillars, had a front court opening onto this circular road. They were only sixteen metres tall and each had one floor fewer than most other Parisian buildings of the time. They were not rented out in the usual way but were instead private hotels occupied by leading bourgeois or aristocratic families. Some of them have them retained their lavish Second Empire decor and have been protected ever since this time. Haussmann, however, considered these buildings too small in relation to the spaciousness of the square. He could not agree with the architects Hittorff and Rohaut de Fleury. Hittorff thought that the effect of the Arc de Triomphe would be lessened if the hotel façades were too big. Napoleon 3rd

The Champs Elysées seen from the Arc de Triomphe in 1845, painting by Jacottet.

View of the Ternes quarter and the Monceau plain from the top of the Arch in 1842.

was very sensitive to the idea of anything detracting from the glory of his uncle, Napoleon Ist, and he sided with the architect.

Eight of these hotels are single fronted, four others are double fronted, in other words twice as big, depending on the amount of space available in the trapeze shape formed by the convergence of the avenues [1].

In his "Mémoires", Baron Georges Eugène Haussmann wrote, with good reason : *"I am proud to have achieved this beautiful layout and consider it to be one of the most successful pieces of work during my time in office."*

Now that work on the Place de l'Etoile had been completed, and the hotels constructed, new avenues opened up converging on the Arc de Triomphe. Work began which would make the existing Champs Elysées Avenue and the Grande Armée Avenue less steep and the remaining landscaping was completed. The Chemin de Ternes was redeveloped and this became Avenue de Wagram, Avenue Chaillot became Avenue Kléber, Avenue de Saint-Cloud became Victor Hugo in 1862 and Avenue de Bezons became Mac Mahon. A further six avenues were to be later created : Avenue de Friedland, originally called Boulevard Beaujon ; Avenue de la Reine Hortense, to become Boulevard de Monceau then Avenue Hoche ; Avenue Carnot, originally named Avenue d'Essling then Prince Impérial ; Avenue Foch, firstly known as Avenue de l'Impératrice then Bois de Boulogne, and finally Foch in 1929 ; Avenue d'Iéna, originally known as Boulevard d'Inkermann ; Avenue Marceau, originally known as Avenue Joséphine before becoming Avenue de l'Alma or Pont de l'Alma, bringing to twelve the number of avenues converging on the Place de l'Etoile.

---

1. These buildings were sometimes, quite wrongly, called the "marshal hotels" because of the neighbouring avenues named after marshals and battles of the First Empire. Napoleon's marshals, of course, never lived in these hotels which were built sixty years after the campaigns of the First Empire. Confusion arises too from a project by Hittorff, eventualy abandoned, to erect statues of the marshals in the square.

The Arc de Triomphe and the Place de l'Etoile around 1890, painting by Chéca Y Sanz.

Left-hand page : The Arc de Triomphe and the Avenue du Bois around 1905, painting by Brancaccio.

The Arc de Triomphe at the end of the Second Empire. Lithograph by Benoist.

L'Etoile rules over different worlds, like living beings. Worlds into which it casts its light. There is the provincial simplicity of Avenue Carnot and the commercial majesty of the Champs Elysées. There is Avenue Victor Hugo... Bérénice used to love dodging from one of these avenues, never remembering which was which, into a side street and out again into the next avenue, just as she would have left a queen for a young girl, a story of knights for a tale by Maupassant. Pathways full of life leading from one part of the imagination to another, Bérénice loved to think of these streets as far off provinces full of the unexpected, or empty alleys with balcony railings as intricately woven as the lives of the people that lived there, she loved too the dubious maze of hotels and rooms, bistros and furtive women all set to send a thrill through perverts and prosperous young men from their rich quarters just a step away. All of a sudden the town would open out and Bérénice emerged from this universe which frightend yet attracted her, to see the Arc de Triopmhe in the distance and leading up to it trees tidily lined up along the railings.

How beautiful Paris is !

Louis Aragon (1897-1982), *Aurélien*.

The Arc de Triomphe around 1910 and 1912: paintings by Eugéne Galien-Laloue.

PROCESSIONS THROUGH THE ARC DE TRIOMPHE

Ever since the ceremony of the official entry into Paris by Napoleon 1st and Marie-Louise of Austria, on 1st April 1810, processions through the Arc de Triomphe have been reserved for the priveleged celebration of national glories or to honour victorious armies. The Return of Napoleon's Ashes in December 1840 was the first real grand ceremony of this kind. The Prince of Joinville, son of Louis Philippe, was ordered to go to Sainte Hélène and to organise the emporer's return. The coffin was landed on the 14th at the Pont de Neuilly. A huge crowd gathered. Many old soldiers of the Grande Armée and the Emporer's unquestioning supporters had spent the night on the Champs Elysées or around the square. "The cold was so intense that some men fell from the branches like ripe fruit", noted Martin Nadeau in his Memoires.

The hearse, drawn by sixteen black horses covered with golden sheets, was parked under the arch overnight from 14th to 15th December. On 3rd August 1842 a funeral procession entered Paris, that of the Duke of Orleans, killed by a fall from his horse at the Ternes Gate near Neuilly. Five years earlier, in 1837, Hélène de Melembourg, who had just married the Duke of Orleans, had made her entrance into Paris passing before the foot of the Arc de Triomphe, in the company of the royal family and members of the government.

"It was terribly cold on 15th December, 1840 when, before daybreak, my father and I went out to perch on the terraces to the left of the Arc de Triomphe, where the only buildings at the time were sheds. From this point we could see right down to the Place de la Concorde on one side and up to the Pont de Neuilly on the other. Never before had there been such a large gathering of people in the streets or public squares and probably there never will be again. All Paris was out of doors. The houses could not have been more deserted had they caught fire. As the procession drew closer, the people in the huge crowd took off their hats and fell silent. My father was fanatical about the Emporer. "Now, he said, I'll be able to leave Paris, my heart's most sincere desire has been accomplished..." and he hastened to leave the following day, never to see the capital again..."

Martin Nadaud, Mémoires de Léonard

"That was the year that the government had Napoleon's remains brought back from Sainte Hélène. Louis Philippe sent his son, the Prince of Joinville, to fetch them. At last the news spread that they had arrived in Le Havre. The boat made its way up the Seine, covered with the insignia of mourning ; the country people lined the banks and a huge crowd gathered to attend the ceremony. I remember that morning perfectly. The cold was intense and the whole of Paris was covered in snow. We were taken to the Hôtel de Flahaut, on the corner of the Champs Elysées. The main lounge was filled with people and ladies in grand mourning dress. We were given a place by a window on the first floor... the view of the Champs Elysées was amazing ; bunches of street urchins were hanging from the trees. The cold caused several to loosen their grips. They fell down into the crowd who let out great yells.

After a wait of more than two hours and a never-ending march-past of national guards, the cortège finally appeared. The hearse represented a grave surrounded by the figures of women. These figures were holding a crown and the whole scene was really beautiful.

Immediately after came Napoleon's old officers, on foot, bare headed and in uniform. My father was one of these and I

Ceremonial entry of Louis-Philippe into Paris. Painting by Thomas Boys.

The Return of Ashes of Napoleon 1st, on 15th December 1840. The funeral procession through the Arc de Triomphe.

could not fail to see the emotion on his handsome face[1]. There was silence as the cortège passed by. The great mass of people, down to even the very coldest, had been overcome by emotion."

Comtesse d'Armaillé, *Mémoires*

On 20th April 1848 the government of the 2nd Republic organised a Fête de la Fraternité, with a huge military march-past, through the Arch.

"It was amidst this extreme confusion of thoughts and feelings, totally devoid of any political or social direction, that the day chosen for this Fête de la Fraternité finally dawned. The sky was overcast. Preparations had been going on to make this a truly magnificent celebration. All morning a population eager to miss nothing had been pouring into the streets. Around two hundred thousand men, national guards, mobile guards, line troops and republican guards had been called up. At nine o'clock, a salvo of twenty-one canon shots announced the arrival of the provisional government on the rostrum of the Arc de Triomphe. From the terraces of an amphitheatre decked out with flags and emblems, which dominated the long, straight, avenue climbing up from the Palais de Catherine de Médicis to join the triumphal monument of Napoleon Bonaparte, the people could see the official representation and the imposing image of their very own sovereign in the distance and they greeted them with cheers. At the top of the rostrum magistrates, army officers, civil servants, delegations, guilds and schools took their places between the two orchestras, whose belted their chords out into the air. A group of elegantly dressed women, each one holding a bouquet of flowers tied up with red, white and blue ribbon, crowned the simplicity of this serious and patriotic occasion like a wreath. Towards 10 o'clock the proces-

The Fête de la Fraternité in 1848 by Champin.

sion set off, it did not finish until very late in the evening."

Marie d'Agoult, *Mémoires*

On 2nd December 1852, Louis Napoleon, proclaimed Emperor following a crushing plebiscite, headed his troops as they paraded through the Arch.

When Victor Hugo died on 22nd May 1885, the Chamber of Deputies decided to organise a national funeral for this poet who had so often slandered Napoleon 3rd. The architect Charles Garnier, then at the height of his success — ten years earlier he had completed the Opéra — was commissioned to design a grandiose, 22 metre high cenotaph which was placed under the arch. A black veil was draped down from the Falguière horses, which were still in place on the left of the monument and veiled flags were placed at the four corners as a sign of mourning. Escutcheons were placed on the square's candelabra on which were written the titles of the poet's works. Huge medallions under the small arches bore the inscription "LA FRANCE À VICTOR HUGO".

Ever since Victor Hugo's national funeral, tributes paid by France to her most valorous have been fairly rare. Included in these, however, were Lazare Carnot

1. Général Philippe de Ségur (1780-1873)

Entry of Napoleon 3rd into Paris. The Cortège in the Place de l'Etoile. Engraving by Benoist.
The funeral of Victor Hugo. The catafalque under the Arc de Triomphe.

who, under the Convention, was responsible for organization of the Victory and whose ashes were exhibited under the Arch in 1889 ; Sadi Carnot, a descendant of the former, President of the Republic assassinated in Lyon in 1894 ; Marshal Mac Mahon in 1893 ; Rouget de l'Isle, whose remains were taken from Choisy-de-Roi cemetery to the Panthéon on 14th July 1914, via the Arc de Triomphe... and Marshals Foch in 1928, Joffre in 1931, Leclerc in 1947, de Lattre in 1952 and Lyautey, brought back from Morocco in 1962.

When Victory was celebrated on 14th July 1919 there could be no question but that a grandiose celebration should take place around the Arch and along the Champs Elysées.

Before the actual parade a huge cenotaph, almost as big as that of Victor Hugo, was set in place under the arch. It had been made by the great artists and wrought iron craftsmen of the day : Jaulmes, Sue and Marc and had, on all four sides, Victories whose wings were those of aeroplanes. It weighed 30 tonnes and was to have remained under the Arch. Clemenceau decided at the last moment, however, that the procession should pass under the triumphal arch and so the heavy monument had to be moved elsewhere.

The procession began with disabled servicemen, Marshals Joffre and Foch opening the march on horseback. Next came the inter-Allied senior commanders ; Pershing who had commanded the American detachments, Douglas Haig, the British, Gillain, the Belgians and Montuori, the Italians. The parade of flags, torn to shreds for the most part, was a very moving moment. For the first time ever, tanks passed through the Arc de Triomphe too. However, one group had been left out of this Victory parade... the airmen. They felt deeply humiliated. As a result, a decision was taken in the Esca-

Charles Godefroy. (Photo Excelsior).

drille bar of Fouquet's to avenge this affront. At 7.30 am of 9th August Airman Godefroy flew under the Arc de Triomphe in his biplane "Newport".

"I will never forget that morning of 14th July 1919. I had spent the night at my father's so I could be at the windows of the Champs Elysées at first light. Even the roofs were packed with children who ran amongst the chimneys and provided the public with anxious diversion. The people of Paris, not wanting to miss anything, had demolished the reserved tribunes : everyone should be down in the street to see the parade of heroes. The sunshine, the military music, the scissor-like legs of the soldiers marching past hour after hour, the flags waving everywhere, the marshals and generals, all formed a glorious seething mass stretching right down as far as the Republic. The squares were

Godefroy's aeroplane flying through the Arc de Triomphe.
Photo from the Excelsior newspaper.

alive with the laughter of bivouacking Parisians and Paris was filled with red, white and blue.

Elisabeth de Gramont,
Les Marronniers en Fleurs.

"I was there for one of the most colourfully red, white and blue days of all time, the Victory Parade of 1919. The huge military parade, the last to pass through the Arc de Triomphe before the stone to the Unknown Soldier was finally laid, was daubed with the colours of all the allies' uniforms. The architects Suë and André Mare had been chosen to decorate the square. A heavy, golden cenotaph designed by Bartholomé, had been kept overnight under the high vault and was set at daybreak in front of Rude's Marseillaise group. Banners fluttered and cockerels stood triumphantly upon pyramids of enemy canons. The sky blue regiments formed long, moving rectangles. Thousands of Parisians spent the night out in the streets to be sure of having a place the following day. Clusters of people hung from the highest chimneys on the Champs Elysées. I was at a window on the corner of Rue Bassano and I spent hours watching the comings and goings of men carrying their long ladders and stepladders, renting out their rungs at inflated prices.

Heel to heel, Joffre and Foch were the first to pass through the Arch to a deafening ovation. Further back, another ovation arose as Pétain rode by alone on his white horse. Throughout the whole morning, until half past twelve, all the troops one could ever imagine flowed past, playing their music, like a rising river and we firmly believed there would never again be a war. The waves of cheering never stopped, and this all lasted for hours. What a wonderful day !"

René Héron de Villefosse, *Souvenirs.*

"They had no difficulty in reaching the immediate outskirts of the Champs Ely-sées... Apart from the bars and a few grocery stores, the shops were closed. Many flags hung in the windows, French, British, American ; flags of all sizes, belonging to each of the allies. In the first rows of the crowd were those people who had spent the night waiting. [...]

They could see, under the Arc de Triomphe, through the dragon spears, the very top of the great cenotaph. [...]

This is when the music starts up. All of a sudden the noise of the crowd dies away as a wave of silence quickly descends the avenue, preceded by a gentle "ssshhh" which ripples quickly along. Every head is bare. The music is deafening, as if the band of every single regiment in France has assembled at the Place de l'Etoile. A sound that pierces your chest, just level with your diaphragm, like an ice-cold blade : the chime to the dead. And the silence of the far-stretching crowd is broken as the sobbing of first one person, then another, is heard above the rest. A large flag is hoisted up the Arc de Triomphe ; it reaches the very top. A rocket whistles, then explodes. The canon booms. The parade is about to start."

Jules Romains,
Les Hommes de bonne Volonté

Among the great contemporary events which have taken place at the foot of the Arc de Triomphe, and which are still remembered by all, is General de Gaulle's homage paid to the Unknown Soldier on his return to France on 25th August 1944, and the parade of Leclerc's 2nd armoured Division.

Since this time, 14th July parades have, with very few exceptions, taken place on the Champs Elysées. However, the different participating corps and armoured or motorized divisions do not pass through the Arch, but instead skirt around it as the parades form and then finish at the Concorde.

Departure of the cortège on 14th July 1919 with the cenotaph in the foreground.

Marshals of France Joffre and Foch at the head of the cortège.

Illumination of the Arc de Triomphe, 11th November 1920. Drawing by Raoul Serres.

"At three o'clock in the afternoon I arrive at the Arc de Triomphe. I relight the flame. Ever since 14th June 1940 no one has been able to do this without the invaders' presence. Then I leave the vault and the terreplein. My assistants move aside. In front of me is the Champs Elysées.

Ah ! It's the sea ! A vast crowd has gathered at either side of the road. Maybe two million souls. The roofs are black with folk. People are packed in tightly at every window, piled up on top of one other, waving their flags. Human clusters are hanging off ladders, poles and street lamps. In the sunshine, as far as the eye can see, there is nothing but a living swell of red, white and blue. I walk on... with every step I take at this most famous of places, I cannot help feeling that the glories of the past are mingling with those of today. Under the Arch the gentle flame burns more brightly in our honour. The avenue, along which our triumphal army marched twenty-five years ago, opens out radiantly before us. As I salute Clemenceau, standing upon his pedestal, he looks ready to leap down alongside us. "

Charles de Gaulle, *Mémoires de Guerre*

General de Gaulle at the Arc de Triomphe on 25th August 1944

The crowd on the Champs Elysées, 26th August 1944, following the Liberation of Paris.

Royal Air Force tribute to the Unknown Soldier, 12th June 1942.

General Leclerc de Hautecloque, Commander of the 2nd BD, Place de l'Etoile on 25th August 1944.

John Fitzgerald Kennedy and General de Gaulle in front of the Tomb of the Unknown Soldier.

THE UNKNOWN SOLDIER

Ever since 11th November 1923 "La Flamme du Souvenir", which war veterans come to salute everyday, has been burning non-stop under the Arc de Triomphe. This flame burns from a big bronze disc decorated with twenty-four swords in the shape of a star, between which laurel leaves have been sculpted in low relief. It was made by the famous wrought iron craftsman Edgar Brandt. Out in front of the flame is a rectangular slab, which bears the inscription :

ICI
REPOSE UN SOLDAT FRANÇAIS
MORT
POUR LA PATRIE
1914-1918

It was in 1916, at the cemetry of Rennes, that François Simon, President of the town's "Souvenir Française" organisation, spoke his prophetic words, asking : *"Why doesn't France open the doors of the Pantheon to one of the unknown combattants who died bravely for his country, with just two words and two dates : "A soldier, 1914-19..." "*

Maurice Maunoury, Deputy of the Eure and Loir, gave his support to this idea, which was causing quite a stir in the newspapers ; the public too was behind it all the way.

On 12th November 1919, one year after Armistice, the Deputies voted in favour of the body of the Unknown Soldier being buried at the Pantheon.

The war veterans, however, were of a different opinion. In their view, a more symbolic place than the Pantheon was needed. The journalist Binet-Valmer launched a new press campaign to have the "Unknown Soldier" buried under the Arc de Triomphe. The President of the Council, Georges Leygues, gave him his support. One year later, on 8th November, 1920, the Chamber voted once again and unanimously agreed on the following text : *"The Pantheon will pay tribute to an unidentified soldier who lost his life in the field of honour during the 1914-1918 war. The transfer of the soldier's remains will ceremonially take place on 11th November 1920. On the same day, the remains of the unknown soldier will be buried under the Arc de Triomphe."*

In the Senate the vote was also unanimous.

The bodies of eight unidentified soldiers were taken from cemetries in Flanders, Artois, the Somme, the Chemin des Dames, Champagne, Verdun and Lorraine. Eight coffins were arranged in the citadel of Verdun, then moved around several times. On 10th November 1920, André Maginot, one of the great war wounded and Minister of Pensions, handed a bouquet of flowers, picked on the battlefield of Verdun, to the youngest soldier of the 132nd Infantry Regiment who was standing guard over the coffins. His name was Auguste Thin. The soldier placed the flowers on one of the anonymous catafalques, thus designating for ever "the Unknown Soldier". The latter was transported that same day to Paris and laid in a chapel of rest, which had been erected at the foot of the Lion de Belfort, Place Denfert-Rochereau. On 11th November, France transfered the heart of Gambetta and the anonymous soldier to their places under the Arc de Triomphe. The cortège was accompanied on its way along the Champs Elysées by 800 flags of all the Allied Armies ; a vast crowd attended the ceremony.

The catafalque was first placed in a low room in the Arch and a guard mounted over it. It was then decided to bury it in a vault under the large arch, facing the Champs Elysées. The ceremony of placing the catafalque in the vault did not take place until 28th January 1921, in the presence of all the government members, the President of the Republic, Marshals

Foch, Joffre and Pétain, delegations of war veterans and Lloyd George, Prime Minister of Great Britain.

This tribute seemed inadequate to the journalist and poet Gabriel Boissy. He put forward the idea of "a real live flame, a flickering fire which would represent the presence of a friend, the unknown soldier, burning as an everlasting reminder to each and every one of us, to the country as a whole."

On 11th November 1923, André Maginot lit the flame of remembrance for the very first time.

Jacques Péricart, a war veteran, then suggested forming a "Comité de la Flamme" with Léon Balby, editor of the newspaper *L'Intransigeant*, whose members would come each evening at 6.30 to symbolically relight the flame.

The flame is relit with the aid of a two-edged sword, which serves to prolong the ceremony. This sword is kept with the head warden of the Arc de Triomphe.

This ceremony continued to take place during the Occupation. Some German soldiers and officers even came to pay tribute to the Unknown Soldier.

The presidents of this committee were, respectively, Generals Gourand (1923) ; Giraud (1947) ; Koenig (1949) ; Balhouard (1951) ; Zeller (1955) ; Beaufre (1971) ; Valentin (1975) and Vaillant (1981)... and today General Liron.

The watchful Flame under the Arc de Triomphe.

A huge French flag floats under the Arc de Triomphe during the visit of foreign heads of state.

Ceremony of the Flame in 1997.

FROM THE PLACE DE L'ETOILE
TO CHARLES DE GAULLE

The hillock of Chaillot, crossroads of Chaillot Hill, officially became "La Place de l'Etoile" by imperial decree on 23rd May 1863, just as the final touches and landscape work were completed.

When General de Gaulle died on 9th November 1970, the Council of Paris voted, on 11th December, to change the name of the Place de l'Etoile to "Place Charles de Gaulle".

In fact, the former name is still the more commonly used and both terms, Place Charles de Gaulle - Etoile, are generally employed.

On the day the mass Requiem was celebrated at Notre-Dame on 13th November 1970, in the presence of eighty heads of state, Parisians still made their way spontaneously to the Arc de Triomphe to pay the General their last respects, even though he had been buried at Colombey.

That same evening, the Council of Paris took a decision with a certain amount of emotion and with total unanimity. One month later, however, this unanimity was no longer reached since, on 13th December, the decision was only voted in by forty-four votes to forty-one...

Edouard Frédéric Dupont, Mayor of the 7th Arrondissement, had proposed replacing the name of Porte de Maillot with that of Charles de Gaulle.

---

1. By the decree of 13th August 1854, passed in Biarritz, Napoleon 3rd outlined the conditions laid down on resident owners of hotels to be constructed regarding garden railings. This decree already used the term "Place de l'Etoile".

The Arc de Triomphe and the Avenue lit up by the Comité des Champs Elysées, created in 1922 and whose symbol is the Arc de Triomphe.

The Arc de Triomphe in 1960.

The Arc de Triomphe is one of the most visited monuments in Paris : 350,000 visitors per year. Having passed though the museum which occupies rooms in the upper section, the public comes to the outer platform, from where is to be had an exceptional panoramic view of the twelve avenues which branch out from the Place de l'Etoile, as well as the whole of Paris.

Open every day : from 1st April to 30th September, from 9.30 am to 11 pm ; from 1st October to 30th March, from 10 am to 10.30 pm. Unaccompanied or guided tours. Closed on 1st January, 1st May and 25th December.

Tél. : 01.55.37.73.77.

A new lift has recently been installed in the south-west pillar.

Since 1924 the Société d'Encouragement has taken the Arc de Triomphe as a symbol for its main annual Grand Prix. Poster by Cassandre.

The "Fête des Moissons" in front of the Arc de Triomphe in 1990.

Illuminations on the Arc de Triomphe in 1998.

The Arc de Triomphe in 1989. Red, white and blue decoration by Catherine Feff.

The Arc de Triomphe and the Place de l'Etoile by Kojiro Akagi.

Acknowledgements

The Publisher and the author's thanks go to Mr. Michel Marot, Architect, Premier Grand Prix de Rome, Architecte en chef des Bâtiments civils et Palais Nationaux, Architecte de l'Arc de Triomphe who has allowed us access to his archives and documents, helped us with his precious advice and been so kind as to write a preface for this historical guide ; Patricia Bailly, Galerie Charles and André Bailly, Galerie Berko (Paris and Brussels), Mr. Claude Abron, photographer, Dominique Clemenceau, Musée du Voyage Louis Vuitton, France-Galop, Kojiro Akagi, Bernard Jeannot, administrateur de l'Arc de Triomphe, and Nathalie Laverroux for the text layout.

Bibliography

Jean-Denis Thierry : *L'Arc de Triomphe*. Firmin Didot.
François de Saint Simon : *La Place de l'Etoile*, Editions Vendôme.
Ariste et Arrivetz : *Les Champs Elysées*, Emile Paul.
Martin Nadeau : *Mémoires de Léonard*.
Alexandre Arnoux : *Féérie des Vingt Arrondissements*.
André de Fouquières : *Mon Paris et ses Parisiens*.
Elisabeth de Gramont : *Les Marronniers en Fleurs*.
Héron de Villefosse : *Le Cœur battant de Paris*, Pont Royal.
Marie d'Agoult : *Mémoires*
Comtesse d'Armaillé : *Mémoires*
Emile Zola : *La Curée*
Louis Aragon : *Aurélien*
Marc Gaillard : *Les Belles Heures des Champs Elysées. Guide de l'axe historique*, Paris au 19e siècle. Editions Martelle, 1990-1996.

Photographic credits

Archives Marc Gaillard, Michel Marot, Catherine Feff.
Photos Claude Abron. Archives Mazda.

From the same author, by the same publisher :

Histoire des Transports parisiens
Les Belles Heures des Champs-Elysées
Paris Ville lumière
L'Eau de Paris
Les Belles heures de Clichy

Collection Guides historiques de Paris

Quais et Ponts de Paris
Quays and Bridges of Paris
Les Fontaines de Paris
Paris, de l'Hôtel de Ville à la Défense
Paris, de place en place

Graphic conception : ENCRAGE, Amiens (03.22.92.64.87)
Printed by Imprimerie SAINT-PAUL à Bar-le-Duc

Dépôt légal : juillet 1998
N° 6-98-1182

I.S.B.N. 2-87890-069-3
© MARTELLE ÉDITIONS
B.P. 0540, 3 rue des Vergeaux
80005 Amiens cedex 1
94 rue Saint-Lazare
75009 Paris